Science

Daily Practice Workbook
20 weeks of fun activities

1st

ARGOPREP

 **Physical Science** •  **Life Science** •  **Earth & Space Science** •  **Engineering**

ArgoPrep is one of the leading providers of supplemental educational products and services. We offer affordable and effective test prep solutions to educators, parents and students. Learning should be fun and easy! To access more resources visit us at www.argoprep.com.

Our goal is to make your life easier, so let us know how we can help you by e-mailing us at: info@argoprep.com.

- ArgoPrep is a recipient of the prestigious Mom's Choice Award.

- ArgoPrep also received the 2019 Seal of Approval from Homeschool.com for our award-winning workbooks.

- ArgoPrep was awarded the 2019 National Parenting Products Award, Gold Medal Parent's Choice Award and the Tillywig Brain Child Award.

SCIENCE SERIES

Science Daily Practice Workbook by ArgoPrep is an award-winning series created by certified science teachers to help build mastery of foundational science skills. Our workbooks explore science topics in depth with ArgoPrep's 5 E'S to build science mastery.

OTHER BOOKS BY ARGOPREP

Here are some other test prep workbooks by ArgoPrep you may be interested in. All of our workbooks come equipped with detailed video explanations to make your learning experience a breeze! Visit us at www.argoprep.com

COMMON CORE MATH SERIES

COMMON CORE ELA SERIES

INTRODUCING MATH!

Introducing Math! by ArgoPrep is an award-winning series created by certified teachers to provide students with high-quality practice problems. Our workbooks include topic overviews with instruction, practice questions, answer explanations along with digital access to video explanations. Practice in confidence - with ArgoPrep!

SOCIAL STUDIES

Social Studies Daily Practice Workbook by ArgoPrep allows students to build foundational skills and review concepts. Our workbooks explore social studies topics in depth with ArgoPrep's 5 E's to build social studies mastery.

KIDS SUMMER ACADEMY SERIES

ArgoPrep's Kids Summer Academy series helps prevent summer learning loss and gets students ready for their new school year by reinforcing core foundations in math, english and science. Our workbooks also introduce new concepts so students can get a head start and be on top of their game for the new school year!

WATER FIRE

MYSTICAL NINJA

GREEN POISON

FIRESTORM WARRIOR

RAPID NINJA

CAPTAIN ARGO

THUNDER WARRIOR

DANCE HERO

ADRASTOS THE SUPER WARRIOR

CAPTAIN BRAVERY

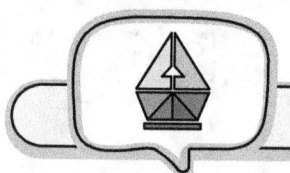

Table of Contents

Introduction

Welcome to our 1st grade science workbook!

This workbook has been specifically designed to help students build mastery of foundational science skills that are taught in first grade. Included are 20 weeks of comprehensive instruction, working through the four branches of science: Physical Science, Life Science, Earth and Space Science and Engineering.

This workbook dedicates five weeks of instruction to each of the four branches of science, focusing on different standards within each week of instruction.

Within the branch of Physical Science, students will study light and sound waves. In Life Science, they will learn more about the external characteristics of plants and animals, as well as how these characteristics help them to survive. Students will dive into the universe and study the patterns of the Sun, moon and stars in Earth and Space Science. Finally, in the Engineering section, they will have the opportunity to become an engineer and design a project aimed at solving a problem in their life.

At the conclusion of the 20 weeks of instruction, students should have a solid grasp on the concepts required of the Next Generation Science Standards for 1st grade.

How to Use the Book

All 20 weeks of daily activity pages in this book follow the same weekly structure. The book is divided into four sections: Physical Science, Life Science, Earth & Space Science and Engineering. The activities in each of the sections align to the Next Generation Science Standards which will help prepare students for state standardized assessments. While the sections can be completed in any order, it is important to complete each week within the section in chronological order, as the skills often build upon one another.

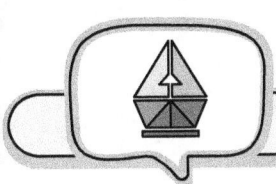
Each week focuses on one specific topic within the section. More information about the weekly structure can be found in the Weekly Planner section.

Weekly Planner

Day	Activity	Description
1	Engaging with the Topic	Read a short text on the topic and answer multiple choice questions.
2	Exploring the Topic	Interact with the topic on a deeper level by collecting, analyzing and interpreting data.
3	Explaining the Topic	Make sense of the topic by explaining and beginning to draw conclusions about the data.
4	Experimenting with the Topic	Investigate the topic through hands-on, easy to implement experiments.
5	Elaborating on the Topic	Reflect on the topic and use all information learned to draw conclusions and evaluate results.

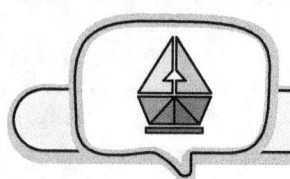
List of Topics

Unit	Week	Topic
Physical Science	1	Vibrations and Sound
Physical Science	2	Communicating over Distance with Sound
Physical Science	3	Light Sources
Physical Science	4	Light Waves
Physical Science	5	Communicating over Distance with Light
Life Science	6	External Characteristics of Animals
Life Science	7	External Characteristics of Plants
Life Science	8	Mimicking Plants and Animals
Life Science	9	Animal Survival
Life Science	10	Trait Inheritance
Earth & Space Science	11	The Universe
Earth & Space Science	12	Patterns of the Sun
Earth & Space Science	13	Patterns of the Moon
Earth & Space Science	14	Patterns of the Stars
Earth & Space Science	15	Seasonal Patterns on Earth
Engineering	16	Identifying a Problem
Engineering	17	Developing a Solution
Engineering	18	Designing a Solution
Engineering	19	Building & Testing Your Solution
Engineering	20	Evaluating Solutions

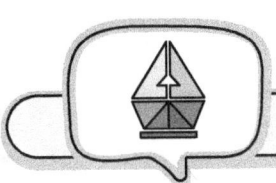
Next Generation Science Standards Correlation Guide

Unit	Week	Next Generation Science Standard	Description of Standard
Physical Science	1	1-PS4-1	Plan and conduct investigations to provide evidence that vibrating materials can make sound and that sound can make materials vibrate.
Physical Science	2	1-PS4-4	Use tools and materials to design and build a device that uses light or sound to solve the problem of communicating over a distance.
Physical Science	3	1-PS4-2	Make observations to construct an evidence-based account that objects can be seen only when illuminated.
Physical Science	4	1-PS4-3	Plan and conduct an investigation to determine the effect of placing objects made with different materials in the path of a beam of light.
Physical Science	5	1-PS4-4	Use tools and materials to design and build a device that uses light or sound to solve the problem of communicating over a distance.
Life Science	6	1-LS1-1	Use materials to design a solution to a human problem by mimicking how plants and/or animals use their external parts to help them survive, grow and meet their needs.
Life Science	7	1-LS1-1	Use materials to design a solution to a human problem by mimicking how plants and/or animals use their external parts to help them survive, grow and meet their needs.
Life Science	8	1-LS1-1	Use materials to design a solution to a human problem by mimicking how plants and/or animals use their external parts to help them survive, grow and meet their needs.

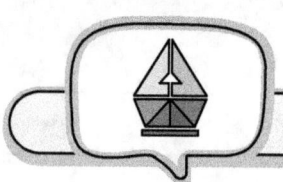

Unit	Week	Next Generation Science Standard	Description of Standard
Life Science	9	1-LS1-2	Read texts and use media to determine patterns in behavior of parents and offspring that help offspring survive.
Life Science	10	1-LS3-1	Make observations to construct an evidence-based account that young plants and animals are like, but not exactly like, their parents.
Earth & Space Science	11	1-ESS1-1	Use observations of the sun, moon and stars to describe patterns that can be predicted.
Earth & Space Science	12	1-ESS1-1	Use observations of the sun, moon and stars to describe patterns that can be predicted.
Earth & Space Science	13	1-ESS1-1	Use observations of the sun, moon and stars to describe patterns that can be predicted.
Earth & Space Science	14	1-ESS1-1	Use observations of the sun, moon and stars to describe patterns that can be predicted.
Earth & Space Science	15	1-ESS1-2	Make observations at different times of year to relate the amount of daylight to the time of year.
Engineering	16	K-2-ETS1-1	Ask questions, make observations and gather information about a situation people want to change to define a simple problem that can be solved through the development of a new or improved object or tool.
Engineering	17	K-2-ETS1-1	Ask questions, make observations and gather information about a situation people want to change to define a simple problem that can be solved through the development of a new or improved object or tool.

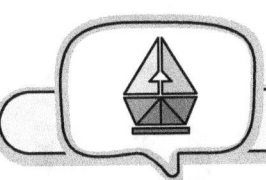
Unit	Week	Next Generation Science Standard	Description of Standard
Engineering	18	K-2-ETS1-2	Develop a simple sketch, drawing or physical model to illustrate how the shape of an object helps it function as needed to solve a given problem.
Engineering	19	K-2-ETS1-3	Analyze data from tests of two objects designed to solve the same problem to compare the strengths and weaknesses of how each performs.
Engineering	20	K-2-ETS1-3	Analyze data from tests of two objects designed to solve the same problem to compare the strengths and weaknesses of how each performs.

How to access video explanations?

Go to **argoprep.com/science1**
OR scan the QR Code:

WEEK 1

Physical Science

Vibrations and Sound

1-PS4-1

Plan and conduct investigations to provide evidence that vibrating materials can make sound and that sound can make materials vibrate.

ARGOPREP

Directions: Read the text below. Then answer the questions that follow.

How Sound is Made

Sound is made when a material **vibrates**, or moves back and forth very quickly. The vibrations create sound waves which can move through air, water and solid objects. Those sound waves can be heard when they reach the ear. With most materials, you can also feel the vibrations. With some materials, you can even see the vibrations.

1. Sound waves are able to move through:

   A. Air

   B. Water

   C. Solid objects

   D. All of the above

2. Vibrations can be:

   A. Heard

   B. Felt

   C. Seen

   D. All of the above

3. .... make sound.

   A. Materials

   B. Solid objects

   C. Vibrations

   D. Movements

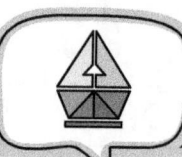
Yesterday, you learned that sound waves are able to move through air, water and solid objects. Today, you will explore how these concepts work.

Directions: Read each text below. Then answer the questions that follow.

Sound Waves and Air

Stretch a rubber band between two of your fingers. With the other hand, pluck the rubber band until you hear a sound.

1. Did you hear a sound from the rubber band?

A. Yes

B. No

Sound Waves and Water

Fill a bucket or large bowl with water. Cut the bottom off a plastic water bottle and place it in the water, cut side down. Put your ear at the top of the water bottle and listen as a family member taps two spoons together underwater.

2. Did you hear a sound from the spoons tapping together?

A. Yes

B. No

Sound Waves and Solid Objects

Create a paper cup and string telephone. Ask a family member to hold one side while you hold the other. Talk to each other through the paper cups.

3. Did you hear a sound through the paper cup telephone?

A. Yes

B. No

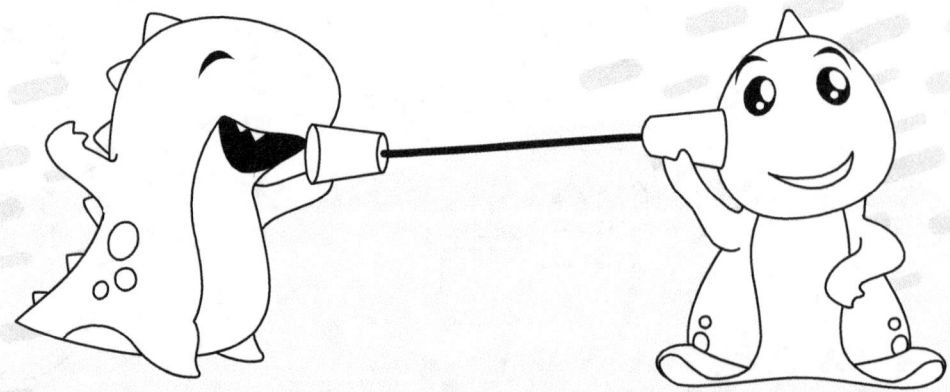

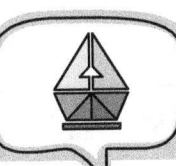
Yesterday, you explored the concept of sound waves moving through air, water and solid objects. Today, you will explain how this is possible.

Directions: Read each text below. Then answer the questions that follow.

Sound Waves and Air

You discovered that a sound is made when you pluck a stretched rubber band.

1. Explain how you think the rubber band makes a sound.

_____

_____

_____

Sound Waves and Water

You discovered that two spoons tapped together underwater creates a sound.

2. Explain how you think the tapping spoons make a sound.

_____

_____

_____

Sound Waves and Solid Objects

You discovered that talking into one end of a paper cup and string telephone really does make sounds that can be heard on the other end.

3. Explain how you think the paper cup and string telephone works.

_____

_____

_____

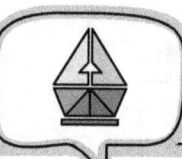
You have spent several days learning about, exploring and explaining sound waves and how they work. Today, you will experiment with creating different sound wave graphs using your own voice.

Materials:

1. Smartphone loaded with a Voice Memo app

Procedure:

1. Open the Voice Memo app on your device.

2. When you are ready, press the red button to begin recording.

3. Record your voice, paying attention to the sound wave graph created with each recording.

4. When you are finished recording, press the red button again.

5. Record your answers for the questions below, repeating, as necessary.

Follow-Up Questions:

1. Draw a picture of what your sound wave graph looks like when whispering.

2. Draw a picture of what your sound wave graph looks like when using a normal talking voice.

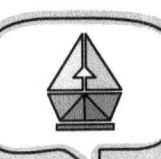
3. Draw a picture of what your sound wave graph looks like when speaking loudly.

4. Draw a picture of what your sound wave graph looks like when screaming.

Yesterday, you collected data while experimenting with voice recordings and sound wave graphs. Today, you will use that data to draw conclusions about sound waves.

Directions: Read and answer each question below.

1. What did the sound waves look like when recording in a quiet voice?

....

....

....

2. What did the sound waves look like when recording in a very loud voice?

....

....

....

3. What can you conclude about the size of sound waves?

....

....

....

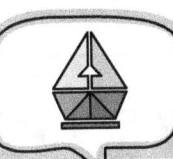
4. When you were recording your voice, was the sound traveling through:

   A. Air

   B. Water

   C. A solid object

5. You know that sound is made by vibrations. When you speak, what do you think is vibrating to make the sound?

....

....

....

6. Why do you think this?

....

....

....

....

Physical Science

Communicating over Distance with Sound

1-PS4-4

Use tools and materials to design and build a device that uses light or sound to solve the problem of communicating over a distance.

ARGOPREP

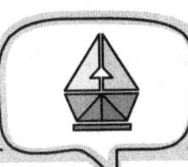
Directions: Read the text below. Then answer the questions that follow.

Sound and Distance

Sound is made when a material **vibrates**, or moves back and forth very quickly. The vibrations create sound waves which can move through air, water and solid objects. Those sound waves can be heard when they reach the ear. Sound waves can travel very far which helps us to communicate over long distances. Think about the siren on a fire truck. When it is turned on, you are able to hear the siren even if you cannot see it.
Animals also use sound to communicate over distances.

1. Sound waves are able to travel long distances.

   A. True

   B. False

2. It is important to be able to communicate over long distances.

   A. True

   B. False

3. You can only hear sounds when you can also see them.

   A. True

   B. False

4. Animals use sounds to communicate.

   A. True

   B. False

5. Sound can be made without vibrations.

   A. True

   B. False

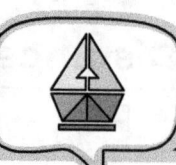
Yesterday, you learned that sound waves are able to travel long distances which is important in helping us to communicate with others. Today, you will explore how this concept works.

Directions: Read the text below. Then fill out the table and answer the questions that follow.

Go outside. Listen to the sounds you hear. Record them on the chart below, along with whether or not you can see the source of the sound being made.

Sound	Can you see the source of the sound?

1. Were you able to see the source of every sound you heard?

   A. Yes

   B. No

2. Were any of the sounds you heard communicating something important?

   A. Yes

   B. No

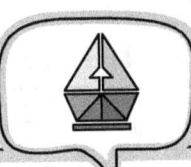
Yesterday, you went outside and listened for sounds, recorded them on a table and decided whether or not you could see the source of the sound. Today, you will explain the importance of the sounds you heard.

Directions: Read and answer each question below.

1. Using the table you made yesterday, list the sounds below that you think were communicating something important.

1.
2.
3.
4.
5.

2. For each sound you listed above, describe why you think it was important.

1.
2.
3.
4.
5.

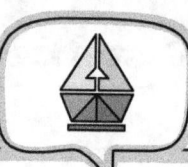
You have spent several days learning about, exploring and explaining how sound waves can travel across long distances. Today, you will experiment with designing and building a device that helps people communicate over long distances.

Materials:

1. A variety of materials found around your home or in nature

Procedure:

1. Brainstorm different devices that could be used to communicate with sound over distance.

2. Sketch your model below.

3. Decide which materials will be used to build your device. Collect necessary items.

4. Build your device.

Sketch:

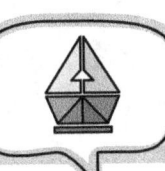
Materials List:

....

....

....

....

....

....

....

....

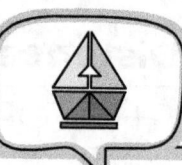
Yesterday, you designed and built a device to communicate with sound over long distances. Today, you will reflect on your device and answer questions about it.

Directions: Read and answer each question below.

1. How did your device solve the problem of communicating with sound over distance?

....

....

....

2. How does your device work? Do the vibrations travel through air, water or a solid object?

....

....

....

3. Did your device work? Why or why not?

....

....

....

4. How could your device be improved upon?

....

....

....

....

Physical Science

Light Sources

1-PS4-2

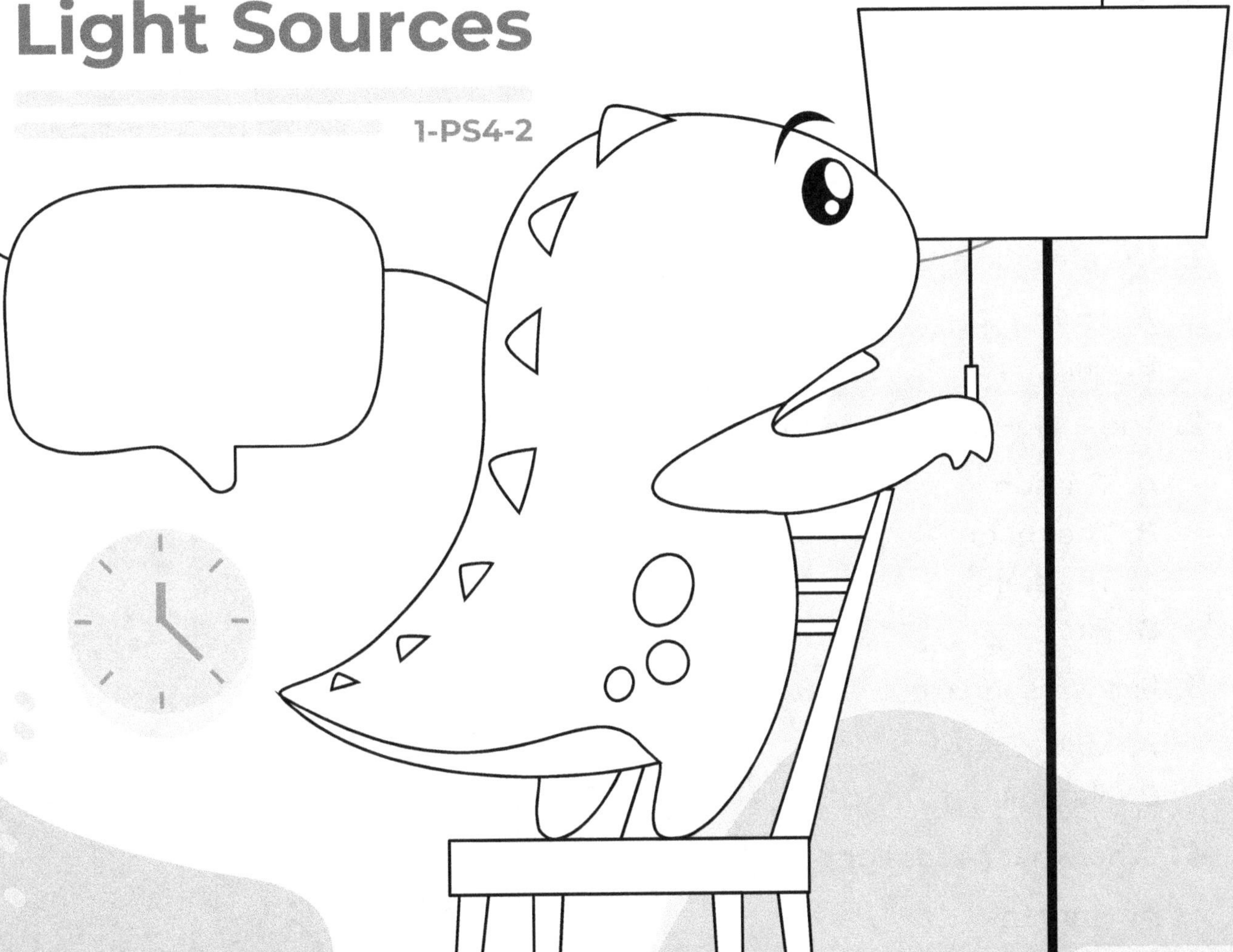

Make observations to construct an evidence-based account that objects can be seen only when illuminated.

ARGOPREP

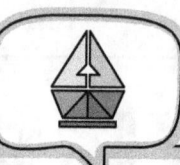
Directions: Read the text below. Then answer the questions that follow.

What is Light?

Light is a type of energy that allows us to see objects in our world. We need light to see. There are many different sources of light. Our main source of natural light is the Sun. Light also comes from other natural sources such as fire and stars, as well as man-made sources such as light bulbs. Light is very important to humans, plants and animals.

1. We are able to see without light.

   A. True

   B. False

2. The main source of natural light is:

   A. The sun

   B. The moon

   C. The stars

   D. Fire

3. Fire is a source of .... light.

   A. Man-made

   B. Natural

4. Who/what needs light?

   A. Humans

   B. Plants

   C. Animals

   D. All of the above

Yesterday, you learned that light is an important type of energy that helps us to see. Today, you will explore how this concept works.

Directions: Read the text below. Then fill out the table and answer the questions that follow.

When it is nighttime, stand in a very dark part of your house (a closet or other room without a window). Look around and think about what you are able to see. Record your observations on the chart below.

Then, turn on the light, look around and observe what you are able to see. Record on the chart below.

Dark Room	Room with Lights

1. Were you able to see anything in the room when it was dark?

    A. Yes

    B. No

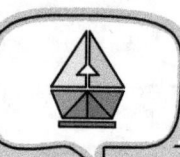
Yesterday, you made observations about what you could see in a dark room and a room with lights and recorded those observations in a table. Today, you will explain the importance of light, based on your observations.

Directions: Read and answer each question below.

1. Draw a picture of the room you were in yesterday and the objects you could see when it was dark.

2. Draw a picture of the room you were in yesterday and the objects you could see when the lights were on.

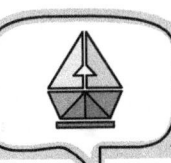
3. What conclusions can you make about light and your ability to see objects?

....

....

....

4. How do you know this?

....

....

5. Do you think light is important? Why or why not?

....

....

....

....

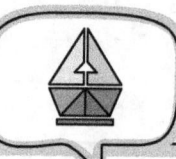
You have spent several days learning about, exploring and explaining the importance of light. Today, you will experiment with creating a pinhole light box.

Materials:

1. A small or medium sized box
2. A small object or toy
3. Tape
4. Pen
5. Flashlight

Procedure:

1. Place the small object or toy in the box (or have your parents put a mystery object in the box for you).
2. Tape the box shut.
3. Use the pen to poke a small hole through one side of the box.
4. Look through the hole. Are you able to see what object is inside the box?
5. If not, experiment with poking other holes in the box and using a flashlight until you are able to see the object in the box.
6. Answer the follow-up questions below.

Follow-Up Questions:

1. How many holes did you poke in your box?

....

....

....

....

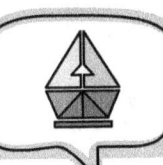
2. Draw a picture of each side of your box below, illustrating the holes you poked in each side.

Top	Bottom
Left Side	**Right Side**
Front	**Back**

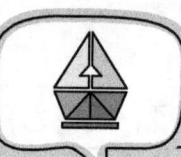
Yesterday, you conducted an experiment with a pinhole light box. Today, you will reflect on the experiment and answer questions about it.

Directions: Read and answer each question below.

1. What did you have to do to finally be able to see the object inside the box?

_____

_____

_____

2. Why do you think you were able to see the object when you did this?

_____

_____

_____

3. What can you conclude about light from this experiment?

_____

_____

_____

_____

WEEK 4

Physical Science

Light Waves

1-PS4-3

Plan and conduct an investigation to determine the effect of placing objects made with different materials in the path of a beam of light.

ARGOPREP

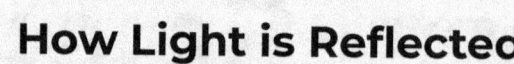
Directions: Read the text below. Then answer the questions that follow.

How Light is Reflected

Light is a type of energy that allows us to see objects in our world. Light waves always travel in straight lines, but objects made of different materials reflect light in different ways. When light reflects off a solid object, we are able to see it. This is because the object blocks the path of the light. Some objects are transparent, or clear, and allow light to pass through them.

1. Light sometimes travels in straight lines.

   A. True

   B. False

2. Different materials reflect light in different ways.

   A. True

   B. False

3. Solid objects:

   A. Block the path of light

   B. Allow light to pass through

4. .... objects allow light to pass through them.

   A. Solid

   B. Transparent

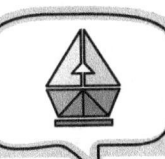
Yesterday, you learned that different materials reflect light in different ways. Today, you will explore how this concept works.

Directions: Read the text below. Then fill out the table that follows.

Objects can fall into one of four categories. These are listed below along with examples.

Opaque: cardboard

Translucent: wax paper

Transparent: plastic wrap

Reflective: a mirror

How do you think light reflects off of each of these materials? Make a prediction on the table below.

Material	Prediction
Opaque	
Translucent	
Transparent	
Reflective	

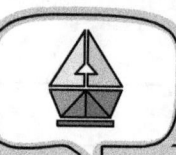
Yesterday, you made predictions about how light is reflected off a variety of materials. Today, you will explain the reasoning behind your predictions.

Directions: Fill out the table below.

Material	Prediction	Reasoning
Opaque		
Translucent		
Transparent		
Reflective		

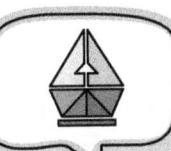
You have spent several days learning about, exploring and explaining how light reflects off objects made of different materials. Today, you will experiment with different materials to test the predictions made in prior lessons.

Materials:

1. An opaque object (cardboard box, cereal box)
2. A translucent object (wax paper, tissue paper)
3. A transparent object (plastic wrap)
4. A reflective object (mirror)
5. Flashlight

Procedure:

1. Test each object by holding it up, placing the flashlight about 5cm away and shining the flashlight toward it. Pay attention to the back side of each object.
2. Record how much light, if any, passes through the object on the chart below. Use a scale of 1-5, with 1 being no light passing through and 5 being the most light passing through.
3. Compare the actual result with the prediction you made for each object.

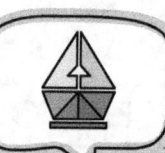
Object	Amount of Light (1-5 scale)	Actual Result vs. Prediction

Yesterday, you conducted an experiment with a flashlight and different types of materials. Today, you will reflect on the experiment and answer questions about it.

Directions: Read and answer each question below.

1. Which material(s) allowed the most amount of light through?

2. Why do you think this is?

3. Which material(s) allowed the least amount of light through?

4. Why do you think this is?

5. What can you conclude about how light travels through different materials?

6. What other materials could you use to test your conclusions?

Physical Science

Communicating over Distance with Light

1-PS4-4

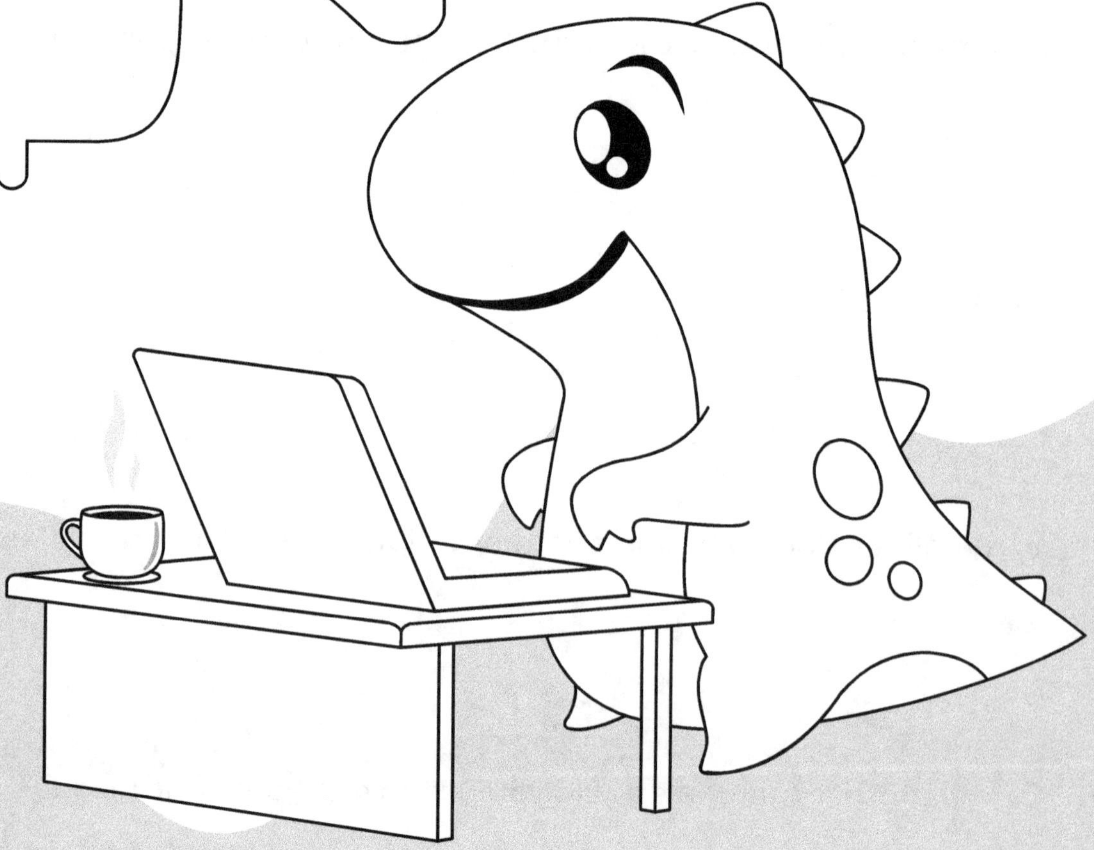

Use tools and materials to design and build a device that uses light or sound to solve the problem of communicating over a distance.

ARGOPREP

Directions: Read the text below. Then answer the questions that follow.

Light and Distance

Light is a type of energy that allows us to see objects when it reflects off them. Even though light always travels in straight lines, different materials reflect light waves differently. Some materials block the path of light and others let light pass through. If there is nothing blocking its path, light waves can travel far which helps us to communicate over distance. Sometimes you may not be able to see the source of the light, other times, you can. Think about a traffic light. The different colors can be seen from a distance and communicate traffic patterns.

1. Light waves are unable to travel long distances.

    A. True

    B. False

2. It is important to be able to communicate over long distances.

    A. True

    B. False

3. Some materials block light waves from passing through.

    A. True

    B. False

4. Light waves always travel in straight lines.

    A. True

    B. False

5. Light can be made without reflection.

    A. True

    B. False

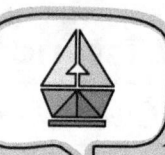
Yesterday, you learned that light waves are able to travel long distances which is important in helping us to communicate with others. Today, you will explore how this concept works.

Directions: Read the text below. Then fill out the table and answer the questions that follow.

Go outside as it begins to grow dark. Look around at the lights you see. Record them on the chart below, along with whether or not you can see the source of the light.

Light	Can you see the source of the light?

1. Were you able to see the source of every light you saw?

    A. Yes

    B. No

2. Were any of the lights you saw communicating something important?

    A. Yes

    B. No

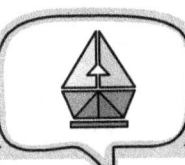
Yesterday, you went outside and looked for lights, recorded them on a table and decided whether or not you could see the source of the light. Today, you will explain the importance of the lights you saw.

Directions: Read and answer each question below.

1. Using the table you made yesterday, list the lights below that you think were communicating something important.

1.
2.
3.
4.
5.

2. For each light you listed above, describe why you think it was important.

1.
2.
3.
4.
5.

3. Do you think all lights are important? Why or why not?

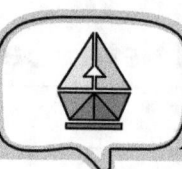
You have spent several days learning about, exploring and explaining how light waves can travel across long distances. Today, you will experiment with designing and building a device that helps people communicate over long distances.

Materials:

1. A variety of materials found around your home or in nature

Procedure:

1. Brainstorm different devices that could be used to communicate with light over distance.
2. Sketch your model below.
3. Decide which materials will be used to build your device. Collect necessary items.
4. Build your device.

Sketch:

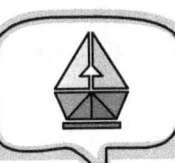
Materials List:

....

....

....

....

....

....

....

....

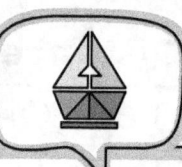
Yesterday, you designed and built a device to communicate with light over long distances. Today, you will reflect on your device and answer questions about it.

Directions: Read and answer each question below.

1. How did your device solve the problem of communicating with light over distance?

....

....

....

....

2. How does your device work? How are the light waves reflected?

....

....

....

....

3. Did your device work? Why or why not?

....

....

....

....

4. How could your device be improved upon?

....

....

....

....

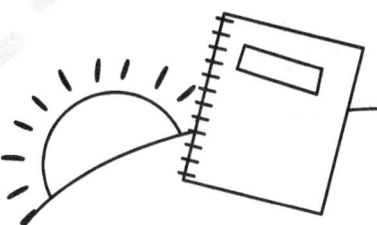

Life Science

External Characteristics of Animals

1-LS1-1

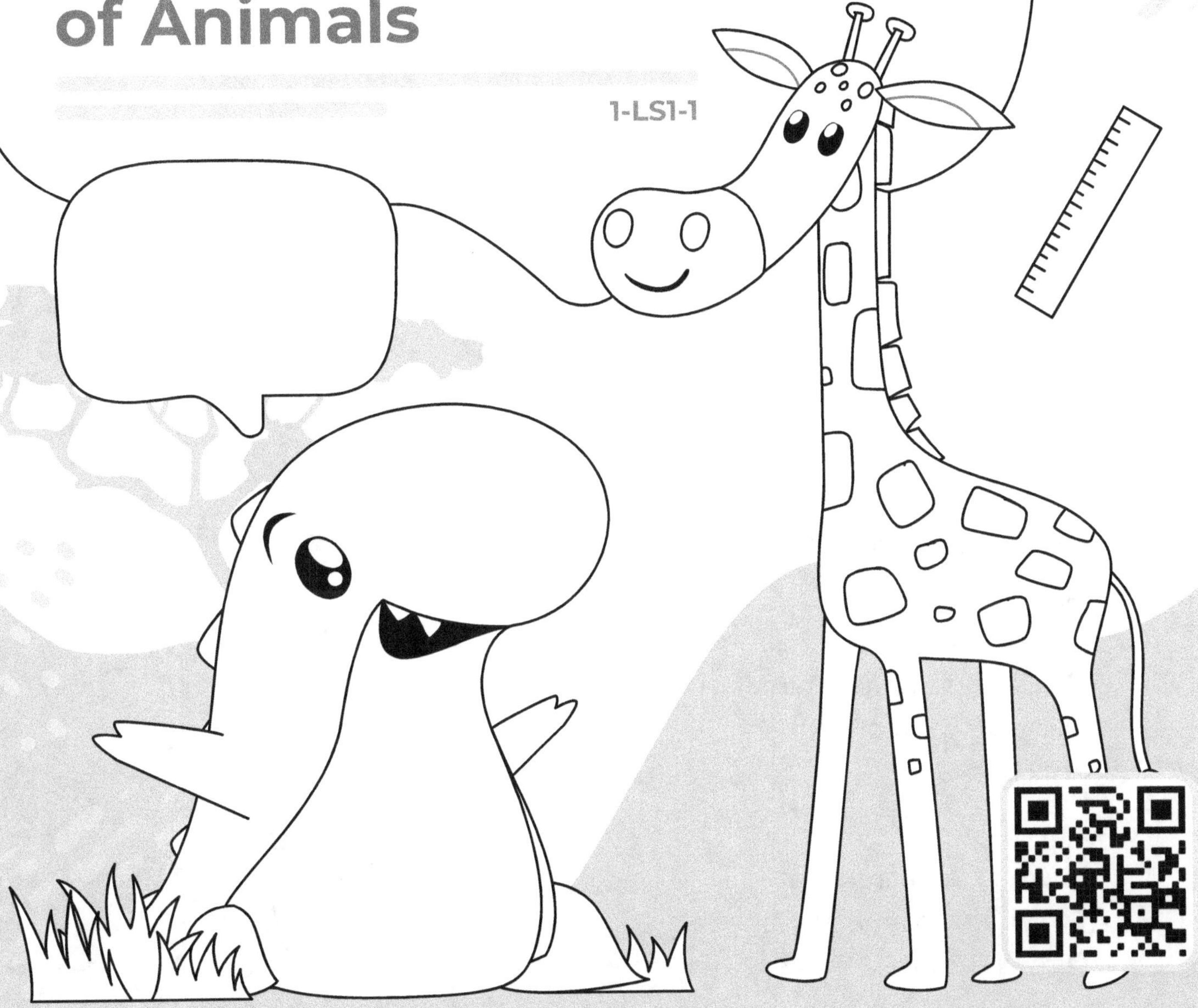

Use materials to design a solution to a human problem by mimicking how plants and/or animals use their external parts to help them survive, grow and meet their needs.

ARGOPREP

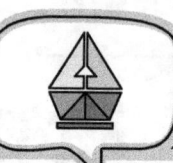
Directions: Read the text below. Then answer the questions that follow.

External Parts of Animals

All animals have **external characteristics**, or body parts on the outside. These parts often help animals meet their needs or survive in nature. This means the body parts might help the animal to find food or escape predators. Think about a bird. The external parts of a bird include: a beak, clawed feet and feathers. Each of these parts helps a bird to survive in its habitat in a different way.

1. External means:

   A. Inside

   B. Outside

2. An example of an external characteristic is:

   A. Heart

   B. Lungs

   C. Fur

   D. Teeth

3. External parts might help an animal:

   A. Find food

   B. Build a nest

   C. Escape a larger animal

   D. All of the above

4. A habitat is:

   A. A nest

   B. An external part

   C. Where an animal lives

   D. A predator

Yesterday, you learned that external characteristics can help an animal to survive in its environment. Today, you will explore how this concept works.

Directions: Read the text below. Then fill out the table and answer the questions that follow.

Go outside and look around for a bird in nature. Observe the bird for as long as possible. List the external characteristics you notice on the table below. Then, draw a picture of the bird, labeling the external parts you listed on the table.

External Characteristics of a Bird	

Sketch of the Bird:

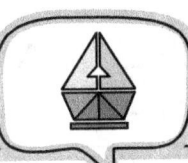
Yesterday, you went outside and observed a bird in nature. You also listed its external characteristics and sketched a diagram. Today, you will explain the importance of the bird's external parts that you observed.

Directions: Complete the table below.

Using the table you made yesterday, list the external characteristics you observed on the left. On the right, describe how that external body part may help the bird survive in its environment.

1.	
2.	
3.	
4.	
5.	
6.	
7.	
8.	

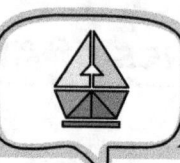

You have spent several days learning about, exploring and explaining how the external characteristics of animals help them survive. Today, you will experiment with this content by comparing and contrasting the bird you observed with other types of birds.

Materials:

1. A computer with internet access or a variety of books about birds

Procedure:

1. Study 5 different birds online or in books.
2. Complete the table below.

Type of Bird	External Characteristics Observed	Is this bird similar to the bird you observed? (yes/no)

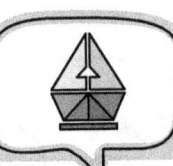
Yesterday, you observed 5 different birds, listed their external characteristics and compared and contrasted them to the bird you observed on a prior day. Today, you will reflect on your table from yesterday and draw conclusions about birds.

Directions: Read and answer each question below.

1. Did all of the birds have the same external characteristics? If not, how were they different?

_____

_____

2. Why do you think the birds had differences in their external characteristics?

_____

_____

3. How might the differences you observed help each bird to survive?

_____

_____

4. What can you conclude about the external characteristics of birds?

_____

_____

_____

Life Science

External Characteristics of Plants

1-LS1-1

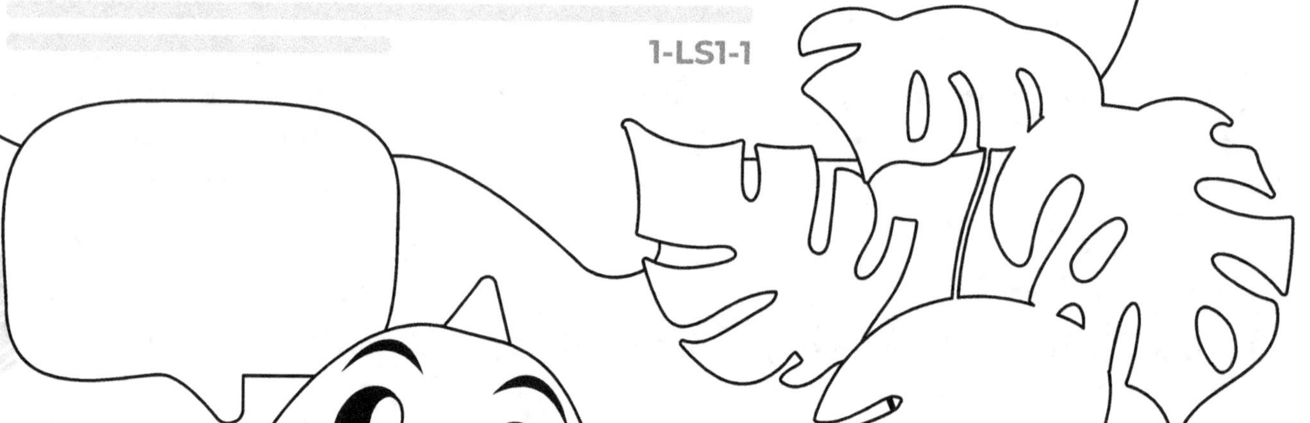

Use materials to design a solution to a human problem by mimicking how plants and/or animals use their external parts to help them survive, grow and meet their needs.

Directions: Read the text below. Then answer the questions that follow.

External Characteristics of Plants

All plants have external characteristics, or parts on the outside. These parts help plants grow, reproduce and survive in nature. Think about a flower. The external parts of a flower include: roots, stem and leaves. Each of these parts helps a flower to grow and survive in its habitat in a different way.

1. An example of an external characteristic is:

    A. Roots

    B. Stem

    C. Leaves

    D. All of the above

2. External parts might help a plant:

    A. Grow

    B. Reproduce

    C. Take in water

    D. All of the above

3. External parts are necessary for plants to survive.

    A. True

    B. False

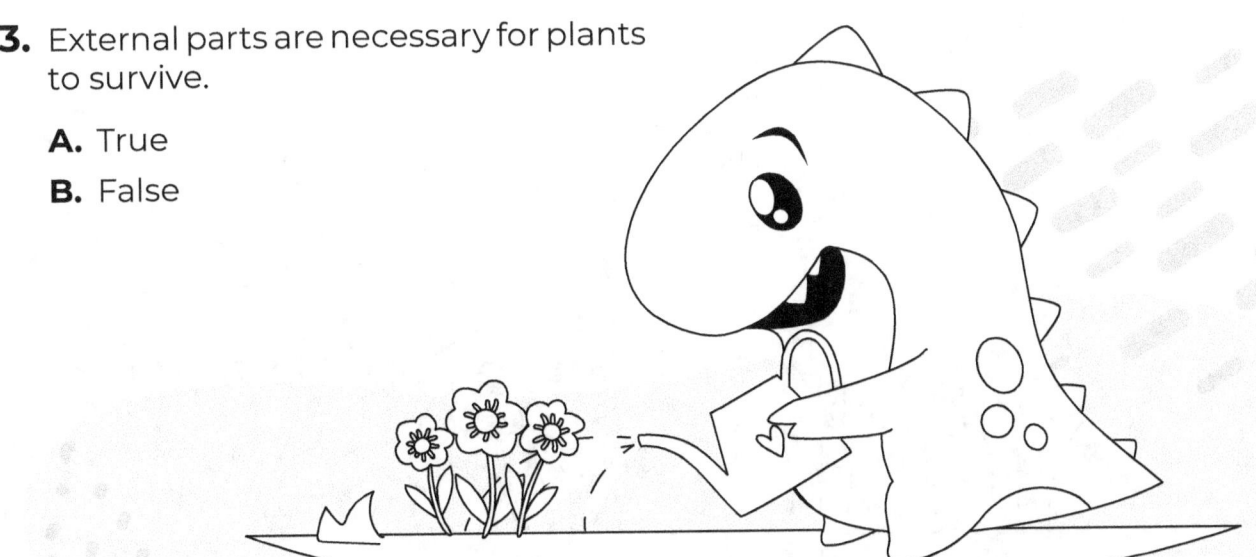

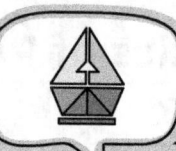
Yesterday, you learned that external characteristics can help a plant to survive in its environment. Today, you will explore how this concept works.

Directions: Read the text below. Then fill out the table and answer the questions that follow.

Go outside and look around for a plant in nature. Observe the plant. List the external characteristics you notice on the table below. Then, draw a picture of the plant, labeling the external parts you listed on the table.

External Characteristics of a Plant	

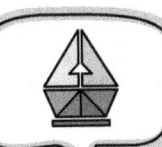
Sketch of the Plant:

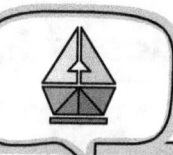
Yesterday, you went outside and observed a plant in nature. You also listed its external characteristics and drew a labeled diagram of it. Today, you will explain the importance of the plant's external parts that you observed.

Directions: Complete the table below.

Using the table you made yesterday, list the external characteristics you observed on the left. On the right, describe how that external body part may help the plant survive in its environment.

1.	
2.	
3.	
4.	
5.	
6.	
7.	
8.	

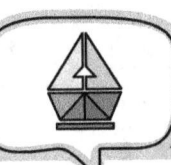
You have spent several days learning about, exploring and explaining how the external characteristics of plants help them survive. Today, you will experiment with this content by comparing and contrasting the plant you observed with other types of plants.

Materials:

1. A computer with internet access or a variety of books about plants

Procedure:

1. Study 5 different plants online or in books.
2. Complete the table below.

Type of Plant	External Characteristics Observed	Is this plant similar to the plant you observed? (yes/no)

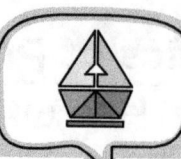
Yesterday, you observed 5 different plants, listed their external characteristics and compared and contrasted them to the plant you observed on a prior day. Today, you will reflect on your table from yesterday and draw conclusions about plants.

Directions: Read and answer each question below.

1. Did all of the plants have the same external characteristics? If not, how were they different?

   ....

   ....

   ....

2. Why do you think the plants had differences in their external characteristics?

   ....

   ....

   ....

3. How might the differences you observed help each plant to survive?

   ....

   ....

   ....

4. What can you conclude about the external characteristics of plants?

   ....

   ....

   ....

Life Science

Mimicking Plants and Animals

1-LS1-1

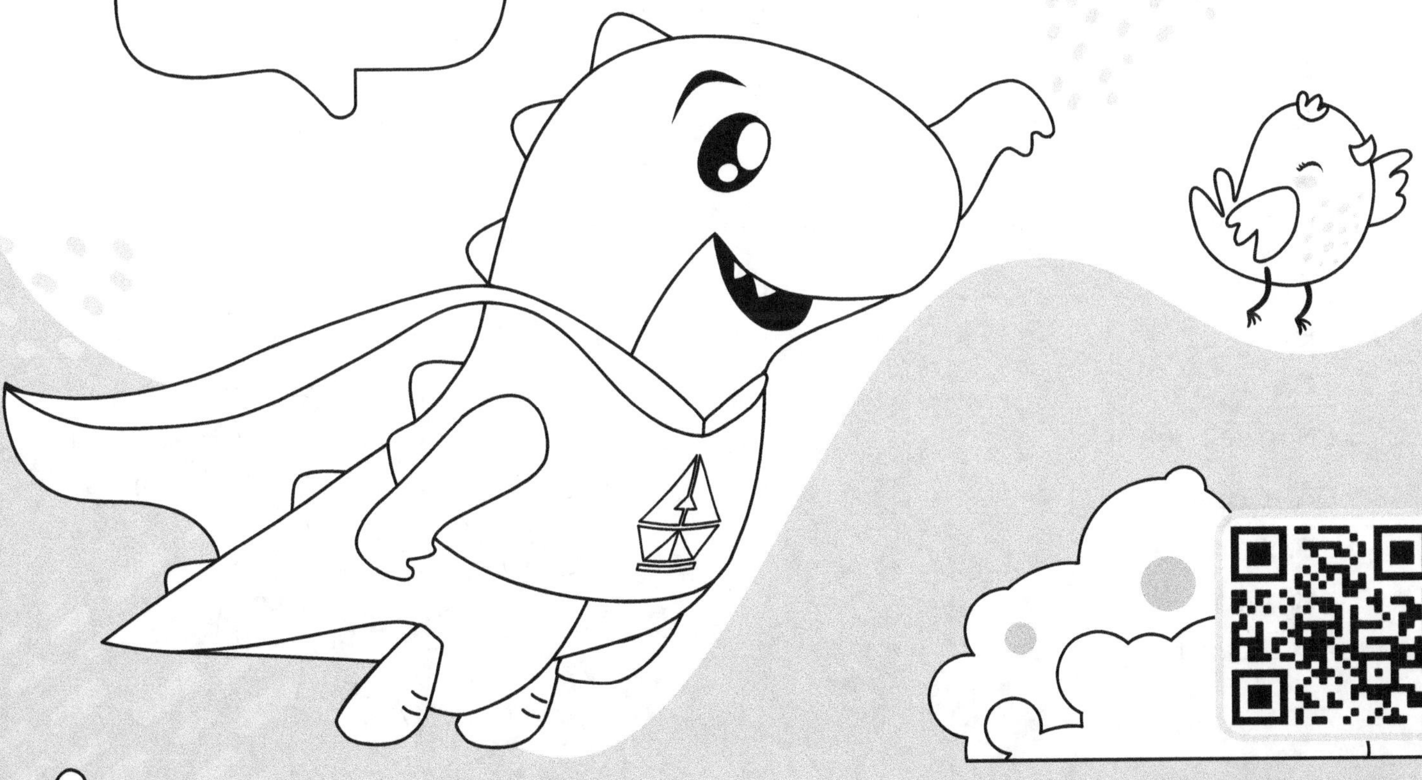

Use materials to design a solution to a human problem by mimicking how plants and/or animals use their external parts to help them survive, grow and meet their needs.

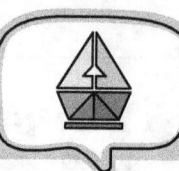
Directions: Read the text below. Then answer the questions that follow.

" Humans Mimicking Plants and Animals

All plants and animals have external characteristics, or parts on the outside. These parts help them grow, reproduce, find food and survive in nature. For instance, a chameleon is able to adapt and blend into its environment. This helps it to hide from predators. Another example is the root system of flowers and other plants. Roots grow deep underground and are very strong to help anchor the plant into the ground. This helps it to survive harsh weather and other elements.

Now think about how these external characteristics of plants and animals might be helpful to humans. Is there a problem that humans face that could be solved by mimicking, or copying, one of the external parts of plants or animals that you have learned about? "

1. List 3 ways external parts are helpful to plants.

    A. ....
    B. ....
    C. ....

2. List 3 ways external parts are helpful to animals.

    A. ....
    B. ....
    C. ....

3. Mimic means:

    A. Copy
    B. Survive
    C. Grow
    D. Adapt

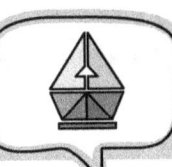
Yesterday, you reviewed how external characteristics can help plants and animals to survive in their environments. You also began thinking about how humans could mimic plants and animals to help solve a problem. Today, you will explore this concept more in-depth.

Directions: Read the text below. Then fill out the tables that follow.

Based on your prior knowledge, list some of the external characteristics of plants and animals you have learned about.

External Characteristics of a Plant	

External Characteristics of an Animal	

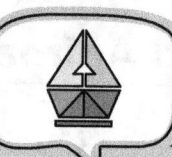
Yesterday, you reviewed the external characteristics of plants and animals that you observed in prior lessons. Today, you will begin to think about how these characteristics could be mimicked by humans to solve a problem.

Directions: Complete the table below.

Using the table you made yesterday, choose 3 of the external characteristics you listed on the left. On the right, describe how that external body part may be mimicked to solve a problem that humans face.

1.	
2.	
3.	

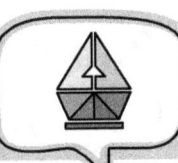
You have spent several days learning about, exploring and explaining how the external characteristics of plants and animals help them survive, as well as how they may be useful in solving a problem humans face. Today, you will experiment with this content by designing a solution to a human problem by mimicking how plants and animals use their external parts to grow, survive and meet their needs.

Materials:

1. Any household material you can access

Procedure:

1. Use the chart you created yesterday to decide which human problem you want to try to solve.
2. Brainstorm solutions that mimic how plants and animals use their external parts to survive.
3. Define the problem and write a short description of your solution below.
4. Draw a prototype of your solution below.

Problem:

....

....

Solution:

....

....

....

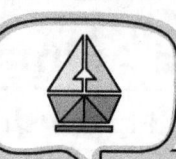
Sketch of your Prototype:

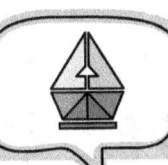
Yesterday, you designed a solution to a human problem by mimicking how plants and animals use their external parts to grow and survive. Today, you will reflect on your design.

Directions: Read and answer each question below.

1. What was the human problem your design addressed?

_____

_____

_____

2. How did your design solve the problem?

_____

_____

_____

3. What plant or animal does your design mimic?

_____

_____

_____

4. After sketching your design, are there any problems with it that need to be addressed (things that would keep it from working)?

_____

_____

_____

_____

Read texts and use media to determine patterns in behavior of parents and offspring that help offspring survive.

Directions: Read the text below. Then answer the questions that follow.

What Animals Need to Survive

All animals have external characteristics, or body parts on the outside. These parts help animals to survive, or stay alive, in their environment. Like humans, animals need food, water and shelter to live. Animals also rely on their parents to help them survive when they are young. Parents might help feed their young, protect them from predators or learn skills they need to survive. Animals are not all that different from humans!

1. Often, an animal's body parts help it to survive in its environment.

   A. True
   B. False

2. To survive, all animals need:

   A. Food
   B. Water
   C. Shelter
   D. All of the above

3. Animals do not need their parents to help them survive.

   A. True
   B. False

4. To survive means:

   A. To find food
   B. Where an animal lives
   C. To stay alive
   D. To have external characteristics

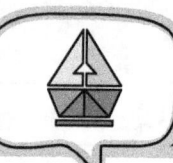
Yesterday, you learned about the things animals need to survive in nature. Today, you will explore this concept more in-depth.

Directions: Read the text below. Then answer the questions that follow.

Young birds rely heavily on their parents to survive in their environment. Choose a bird to research. Use online resources to find out how parents care for their offspring.

1. Type of Bird:

2. What do baby birds need to survive?

3. How do their parents help care for them?

4. How do baby birds communicate their needs to their parents?

5. How do their parents respond? What do they do?

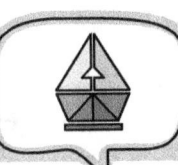
Yesterday, you researched a type of bird and learned about its needs and how those needs are met. Today, you will explain the importance of parents caring for their offspring.

Directions: Answer the questions below, using the information you learned yesterday during your research.

1. Why is it important that parents care for their offspring in nature?

_____

_____

_____

2. Draw a picture below of what it might look like for a parent to care for a baby bird.

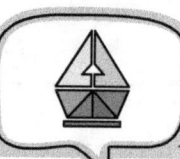
You have spent several days learning about, exploring and explaining how animal parents help their offspring to survive. Today, you will experiment with this content by comparing and contrasting the bird you researched with humans.

Materials:

1. A computer with internet access or an informational book about birds

Procedure:

1. Conduct additional research on birds online or in books, if necessary.
2. Answer the questions below.

Follow-Up Questions:

1. How are baby birds and human babies similar to one another?

....

....

....

....

....

2. How are bird parents and human parents similar to one another?

....

....

....

....

....

....

....

....

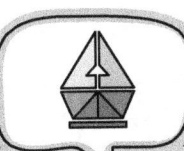
Yesterday, you compared and contrasted birds and humans. Today, you will reflect on the research you've done and draw conclusions about how birds and their needs are similar or different from other animals.

Directions: Read and answer each question below.

1. How do you think the needs of baby birds are similar to those of other baby animals?

....
....
....
....

2. How do you think the needs of baby birds are different from those of other baby animals?

....
....
....
....

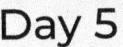

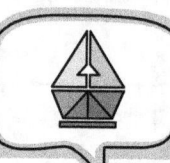
3. How do you think bird parents are similar to other animal parents in how they care for their offspring?

....

....

....

....

....

4. How do you think bird parents are different from other animal parents in how they care for their offspring?

....

....

....

....

....

WEEK 10

Life Science

Trait Inheritance

1-LS3-1

Make observations to construct an evidence-based account that young plants and animals are like, but not exactly like, their parents.

ARGOPREP

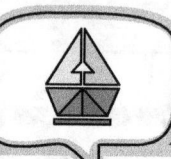
Directions: Read the text below. Then answer the questions that follow.

What is Trait Inheritance?

All plants and animals have traits, or physical characteristics, that make them unique. These might include hair color, eye color and height. Traits are usually inherited, or passed down, from grandparents or parents to their offspring. Think about your own physical traits. Which traits did you inherit from your mom? Which traits did you inherit from your dad?

1. Traits are what make plants and animals unique.

   A. True

   B. False

2. Examples of traits include:

   A. Eye color

   B. Hair color

   C. Height

   D. All of the above

3. Inherited means:

   A. Passed down from a family member

   B. Something that makes a plant or animal unique

4. Plants and animals can only inherit traits from their parents.

   A. True

   B. False

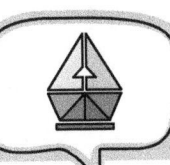
Yesterday, you learned about trait inheritance. Today, you will explore how this concept works.

Directions: On the table below, list 5 traits that make you unique. Then, place an X in the box under the family member you think the trait was passed down from. To decide, think about which family members have similar traits. After you have completed the table, answer the question that follows.

Trait	Mother	Father	Grandparent	Not Sure

1. Do you think you think you look most like your mom or dad? Why?

_____

_____

_____

_____

_____

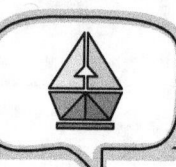
Yesterday, you listed some of your own traits and from whom you think they were passed down. Today, you will explain how plants and animals can look similar to, but not exactly like, their parents.

Directions: Answer the questions below.

1. Do all plants and animals look EXACTLY like their parents?

   ....

   ....

2. Explain how biological factors such as plants and animals affect where people live.

   ....

   ....

3. Sketch a picture of yourself and another picture of one of your parents below.

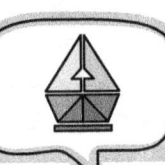
4. In what ways are you similar?

....

....

....

....

....

....

5. In what ways are you different?

....

....

....

....

....

....

You have spent several days learning about, exploring and explaining how plants and animals look similar to, but not exactly like, their parents. Today, you will experiment with this content by expanding your observations to other plants and animals.

Materials:

1. A computer with internet access or an informational book about animal babies

Procedure:

1. Conduct research on plant or animal babies and their parents.
2. Answer the questions below.

Follow-Up Questions:

Plant/Animal Baby	Plant/Animal Parent

Yesterday, you sketched a picture of a plant or animal baby and its parent, based on your research. Today, you will reflect on the research you've done and draw conclusions about how plant and animal babies and their parents are similar to humans and their offspring.

Directions: Read and answer each question below.

1. What plant or animal did you research?

_____

_____

2. Did the plant or animal parent and offspring look EXACTLY alike?

_____

_____

3. In what ways were the plant or animal parent and their offspring similar?

_____

_____

4. In what ways were the plant or animal parent and their offspring different?

_____

_____

5. What can you conclude about the characteristics of plants and animals and their offspring?

_____

_____

_____

WEEK 11

Earth & Space Science

The Universe

1-ESS1-1

Use observations of the sun, moon and stars to describe patterns that can be predicted.

ARGOPREP

Directions: Read the text below. Then answer the questions that follow.

How Big is the Universe?

The universe is made up of everything that exists in space, including all the galaxies, planets, the Sun, moon and stars. Scientists think the universe is 13-14 billion years old. No one really knows how big the universe is, but scientists believe it is expanding, or getting bigger. Our galaxy, the Milky Way, and our planet, Earth, are just very tiny parts of the universe.

1. The universe is made up of:

   A. Galaxies

   B. Planets

   C. Stars

   D. All of the above

2. The universe is at least 13 billion years old.

   A. True

   B. False

3. Expanding means:

   A. Getting smaller

   B. Getting bigger

   C. Staying the same size

4. Our galaxy, the Milky Way, makes up a large part of the universe.

   A. True

   B. False

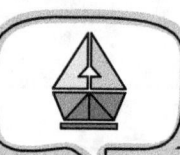
Yesterday, you learned some basic information about the universe. Today, you will explore this concept more in-depth.

Directions: Read the text below. Then answer the questions that follow.

The universe is made up of many different things. Some are very large, while others are much smaller. See the chart below for more information about what makes up the universe, from largest to smallest in size.

Universe	All of the things in space
Galaxy	Many solar systems put together make up a galaxy
Solar System	A central star and the planets that revolve around it
Stars	Huge, glowing balls of gas that give off light and heat
Planets	Large, natural objects that travel around stars
Moons	Natural, rocky object that travels around planets
Asteroids	Chunks of rock and metal of varying sizes that travel around the Sun

Read each description. Write the correct part of the universe on the line.

1. Everything in space ....

2. The Earth, Sun and other planets ....

3. Mercury, Earth, Mars and Jupiter ....

4. A source of light to Earth at night ....

5. Ours is called the Milky Way ....

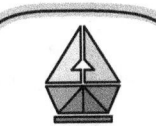
MERCURY

VENUS

EARTH

MARS

JUPITER

SATURN

URANUS

NEPTUNE

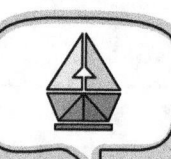
Yesterday, you learned more about what makes up the universe. Today, you will explain how our solar system is just one small piece of the entire universe.

Directions: Answer the questions below. Use the internet or books, as necessary.

1. What makes up our solar system?

....

....

....

2. Our solar system is part of what galaxy?

....

....

....

3. How many galaxies are there in the universe?

....

....

....

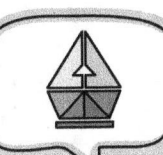
4. Sketch a picture below of what you think the universe might look like. Be sure to include our solar system, as well as the elements you have learned about in previous days.

You have spent several days learning about, exploring and explaining how large the universe is, as well as the elements that are part of it. Today, you will experiment with this content by creating a fun slime model of the universe and its trillions of galaxies.

Materials:

1. Clear glue
2. Borax
3. Water
4. Red and blue food coloring
5. Bowls
6. Measuring cups
7. Glitter
8. Wax paper

Procedure:

1. In one bowl, mix $\frac{1}{2}$ cup glue with $\frac{1}{2}$ cup water. Mix well.
2. Add food coloring and mix to get a deep purple color.
3. In another bowl, mix 1 teaspoon Borax with 1 cup lukewarm water. Stir until completely dissolved.
4. Slowly add the glue mixture to the Borax and water and stir. You may need to use your hands to mix well.
5. Remove the slime from the bowl and put on a piece of wax paper.
6. Flatten the slime and add some glitter on top. Fold it over and press to lock in the glitter. Repeat several times to mix it thoroughly.
7. Store in a sealed sandwich bag.

Follow-Up Questions:

1. What does the slime represent?

2. What does the glitter represent in the slime?

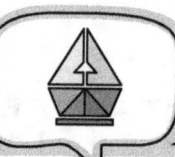
Yesterday, you created a model of the universe by making slime. Today, you will reflect on all that you've learned this week about the universe.

Directions: Read and answer each question below.

1. What is one thing you already knew about the universe or space prior to this week?

_____

_____

_____

2. What are 3 new things you learned this week about the universe and the other elements that are part of it?

A. _____

B. _____

C. _____

3. What are 3 things you are still wondering about and would like to know more about?

A. _____

B. _____

C. _____

Earth & Space Science

Patterns of the Sun

1-ESS1-1

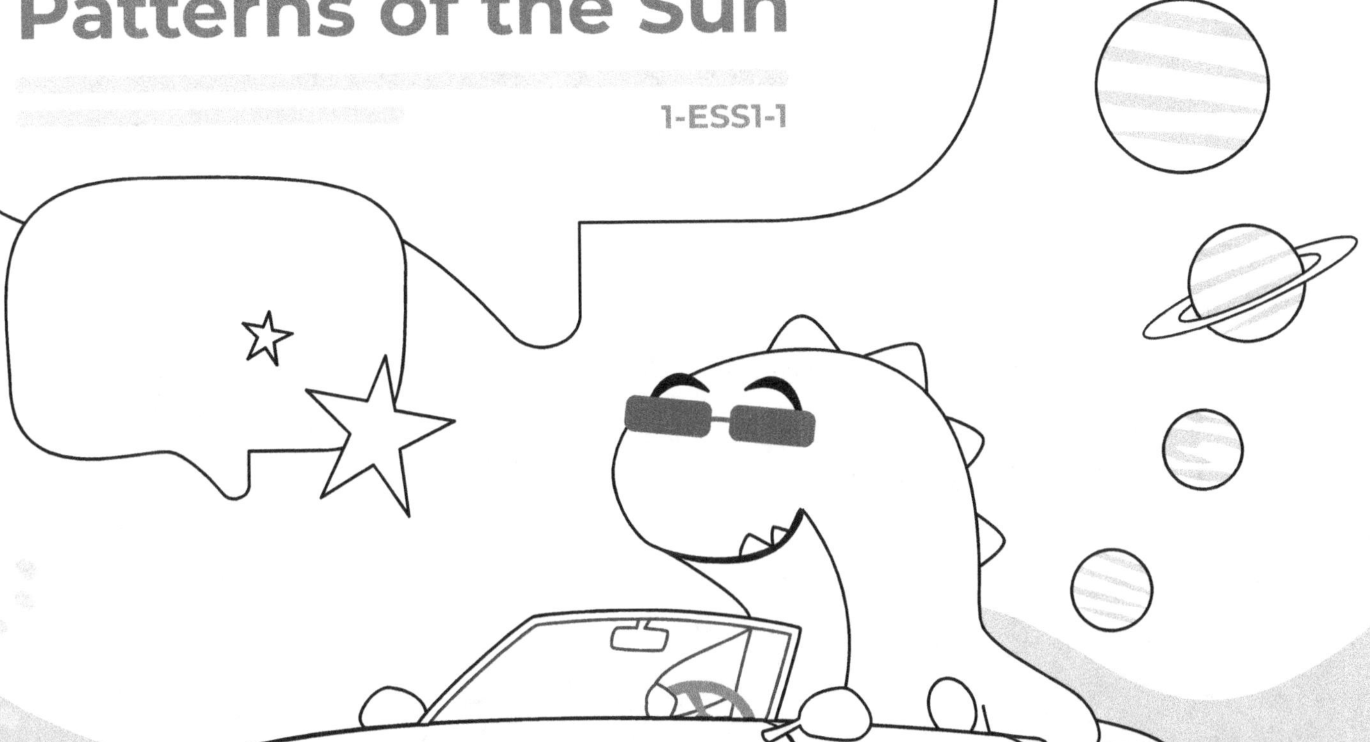

Use observations of the sun, moon and stars to describe patterns that can be predicted.

ARGOPREP

Directions: Read the text below. Then answer the questions that follow.

What is the Sun?

The Sun is the largest and brightest star and is at the center of our solar system. It is a hot ball of gases that gives off a lot of energy. The Sun is an important source of light and heat for the Earth. All of the other objects in the solar system, including the planets, orbit, or rotate, around the Sun.

1. The Sun is at the center of our solar system.

   A. True

   B. False

2. The Sun is:

   A. The largest star in our solar system

   B. The brightest star in our solar system

   C. A source of light and heat

   D. All of the above

3. Orbit means:

   A. To give off light

   B. To give off heat

   C. To go around

4. The Sun is made of water

   A. True

   B. False

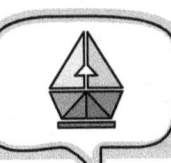
Yesterday, you learned some basic information about the Sun. Today, you will make observations of the Sun to explore this concept more in-depth.

Directions: Complete the table below by observing and recording information about the Sun at 4 different times throughout the day (morning, afternoon, evening, night). Then answer the questions that follow.

Time	Position or Sketch of the Sun (low east, high east, high west, low west)	Night or Day?

1. What did you notice about the Sun throughout the day?

_____

_____

_____

2. Why do you think that happened?

_____

_____

_____

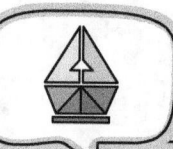
Yesterday, you observed the Sun throughout the day. Today, you will learn more about the pattern of the Sun in order to explain what causes day and night on Earth.

Directions: : Read the text and review the diagram below. Then answer the questions that follow.

The Earth constantly rotates, or spins, as it orbits around the Sun. Each rotation takes 24 hours. The spinning of the Earth is what makes the Sun appear to move across the sky. The Sun shines light on half of the Earth at any given time. When the Sun is shining on your part of the Earth, it is day. When the Sun is shining on the other half of the Earth, it is night.

Review the diagram below of the Earth and sun. Notice that only half of the Earth can be lit by the Sun at any given time.

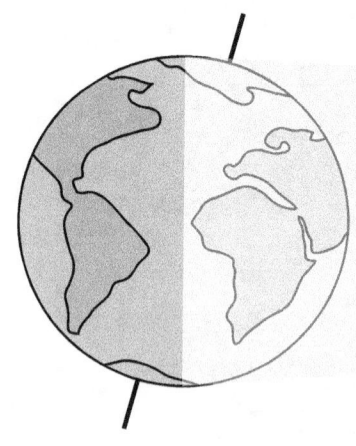

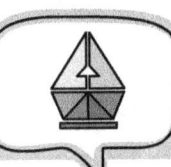
Follow-Up Questions:

1. Yesterday, when making your observations of the Sun, did it appear the Sun was moving across the sky throughout the day?

....

....

....

....

....

2. Was the Sun actually moving across the sky? If not, what was moving?

....

....

....

....

....

3. How does the spinning of the Earth affect our day and night times?

....

....

....

....

....

....

....

....

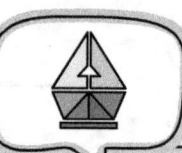
You have spent several days learning about, exploring and explaining how the patterns of the Sun result in daytime and nighttime on Earth. Today, you will experiment with this content by creating a model of the Sun, Earth and moon.

Materials:

1. Any household materials you would like to use (for example: a shoebox, styrofoam balls, string, paint, clay, etc.)

Procedure:

1. Use the materials you have chosen to create a model of the Sun, Earth and moon. Your model should show how only half of our planet can get light from the Sun at any given time.

2. Answer the follow-up questions below.

Follow-Up Questions:

1. Write a short summary below that explains how your model represents the pattern of the Sun and how this pattern affects daytime and nighttime on Earth.

....

....

....

....

....

....

....

....

....

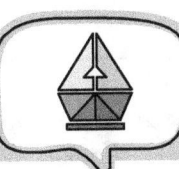
Yesterday, you created a model of the Sun, Earth and moon. Today, you will reflect on all that you've learned this week about the pattern of the Sun.

Directions: Read and answer each question below.

1. Can the pattern of the Sun be predicted from day to day? Why or why not?

2. What does the Earth do that causes daytime and nighttime?

3. Why can we not see the Sun at night?

4. Why can we usually not see the moon during the day?

5. What are 2 new things you learned this week?

    A.

    B.

WEEK 13

Earth & Space Science

Patterns of the Moon

1-ESS1-1

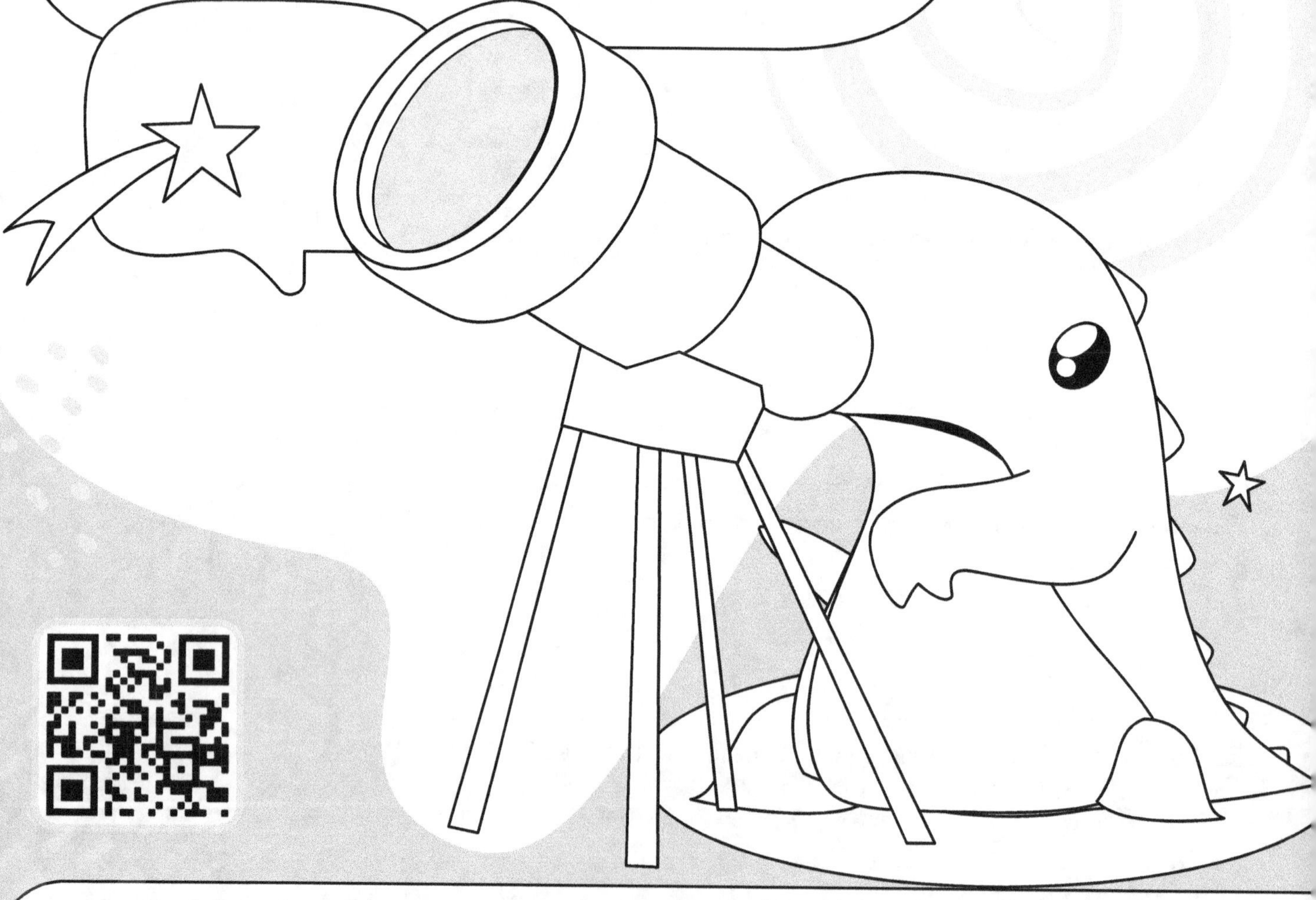

Use observations of the sun, moon and stars to describe patterns that can be predicted.

ARGOPREP

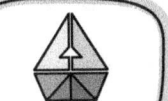
Directions: Read the text below. Then answer the questions that follow.

What is the Moon?

The moon is the second brightest object in our solar system, after the Sun. It is made up of mostly rock. The moon orbits, or rotates around, the Earth. Each trip around our planet takes about 27 days.

1. The moon is at the center of our solar system.

   A. True
   B. False

2. The moon is:

   A. The largest object in our solar system
   B. The brightest object in our solar system
   C. The second brightest object in our solar system

3. The moon orbits:

   A. Earth
   B. The Sun
   C. The universe

4. The moon is made of:

   A. Water
   B. Rock
   C. Gases
   D. Minerals

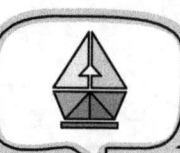
Yesterday, you learned some basic information about the moon. Today, you will make observations of the moon to explore this concept more in-depth.

Directions: Complete the table below by observing and recording information about the moon over the course of 7 days. Then answer the questions that follow.

Day	Sketch of the Moon
1.	
2.	
3.	
4.	
5.	
6.	
7.	

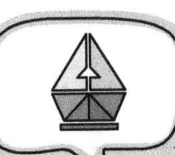
Follow-Up Questions:

1. What did you notice about the moon throughout the week?

....

....

....

....

2. Why do you think that happened?

....

....

....

....

Previously, you observed the moon throughout the week. Today, you will learn more about the pattern of the moon in order to explain what causes us to see different portions of the moon each night.

Directions: Read the text below. Then answer the questions that follow.

You probably noticed in your observations that the moon looks a little different every night. Sometimes you can see the entire moon, and at other times, you can only see a slice of it. Does the shape of the moon change? No, it only appears that way from Earth. The moon reflects light from the Sun. As the moon orbits the Earth, the Sun shines on different parts of the moon, making those parts visible to people on Earth. The different shapes of the moon that we are able to see are called the phases of the moon.

Follow-Up Questions:

1. When making your observations of the moon, did you notice that the moon was a slightly different shape each night?

    ....

    ....

2. Was the moon actually changing shape each night? If not, why did it appear different each night?

    ....

    ....

    ....

3. How does the spinning of the moon affect how much of the moon we are able to see?

    ....

    ....

    ....

    ....

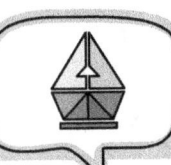
You have spent several days learning about, exploring and explaining how the patterns of the moon result in it appearing to be different shapes each night. Today, you will experiment with this content by creating a model of the phases of the moon.

Materials:

1. Chocolate cream sandwich cookies
2. Paper plate or large piece of white paper
3. Knife
4. Marker
5. Internet access

Procedure:

1. Use the internet to research the 8 different phases of the moon.
2. In the middle of the plate or paper, draw a circle to represent the Earth.
3. Use the sandwich cookies to create a model of these phases. You will need to pull apart the two sides of the cookie. Then, use the knife to scrape off the correct amount of cream so that it represents the moon during that phase.
4. Arrange the cookies in the correct order around the Earth.
5. Answer the follow-up questions below.

Follow-Up Questions:

1. Write a short summary below that explains how your model represents the phases of the moon.

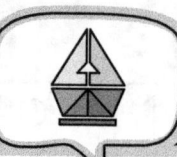
Yesterday, you created a model of the phases of the moon. Today, you will reflect on all that you've learned this week about the patterns of the moon.

Directions: Read and answer each question below.

1. Can the pattern of the moon be predicted from day to day? Why or why not?

....

....

....

2. What does the moon do that causes us to see different portions of it each night?

....

....

....

....

3. Why can we not see the moon during the day?

....

....

....

....

4. What are 3 new things you learned this week?

A. ....

....

B. ....

....

C. ....

....

WEEK 14

Earth & Space Science

Patterns of the Stars

1-ESS1-1

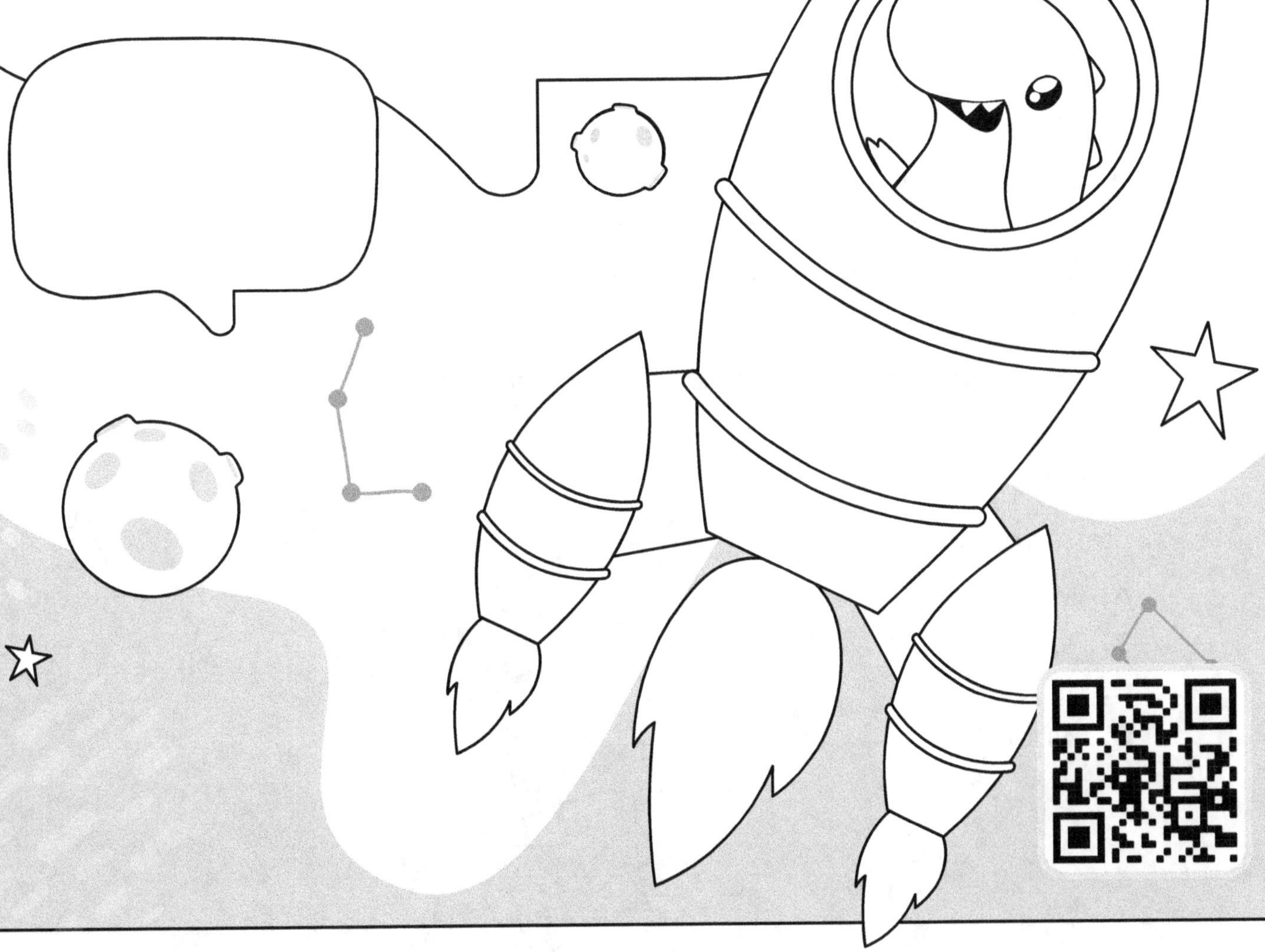

Use observations of the sun, moon and stars to describe patterns that can be predicted.

ARGOPREP

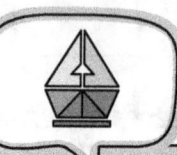
Directions: Read the text below. Then answer the questions that follow.

What are the Stars?

Stars are large, glowing balls of gas. The closest star to the Earth is the Sun. It is also the brightest star that can be seen from Earth. Billions of other stars can be seen as small dots of light in the night sky. These stars are much further away than the Sun. Some stars are so far away that a telescope is needed to even see them.

1. There are thousands of stars in the galaxy.

   A. True

   B. False

2. Stars are:

   A. Glowing balls of gas

   B. Small dots of light in the night sky

   C. So far away from Earth, some can only be seen through a telescope

   D. All of the above

3. The Sun is the brightest star that can be seen from Earth.

   A. True

   B. False

4. Stars are made of:

   A. Water

   B. Rock

   C. Gas

   D. Minerals

Yesterday, you learned some basic information about stars. Today, you will make observations of stars to explore this concept more in-depth.

Directions: Complete the table below by observing the stars during the day and at night. Draw pictures of what you observe. Then answer the questions that follow.

Daytime Sky	Nighttime Sky

Follow-Up Questions:

1. What did you notice about stars during the day?

_____

_____

_____

2. What did you notice about stars at night?

_____

_____

_____

_____

_____

_____

_____

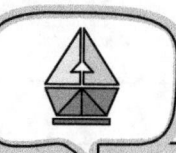
Yesterday, you observed the stars during the day and at night. Today, you will learn more about the pattern of the stars in order to explain why we are only able to see stars at night.

Directions: Read the text below. Then answer the questions that follow.

You probably noticed in your observations that, other than the Sun, the stars are only visible at night. What happens to the stars during the day? Do they just disappear? No, most stars are just not bright enough to be seen during the day. The light from the Sun makes it seem like the other stars disappear, but really they are always in the sky - even during the day.

Follow-Up Questions:

1. When making your observations of the stars, did you notice that they were only visible at night?

2. Did the stars actually disappear during the day? If not, why can we not see them?

3. Why do you think some stars appear brighter than others in the night sky?

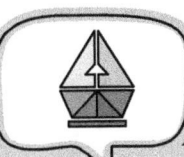

You have spent several days learning about, exploring and explaining how the patterns of the stars result in them only being visible at night. Today, you will experiment with this content by creating a simulation.

Materials:

1. A closet or other dark room with a light
2. A flashlight

Procedure:

1. Go into the closet or dark room. Be sure the lights are out. This represents nighttime.
2. Turn on the flashlight and shine it at the ceiling. This light represents the stars.
3. Leaving the flashlight on, turn on the light in the room. This light represents the Sun (or daytime).
4. Notice whether or not the stars can be seen during the day.

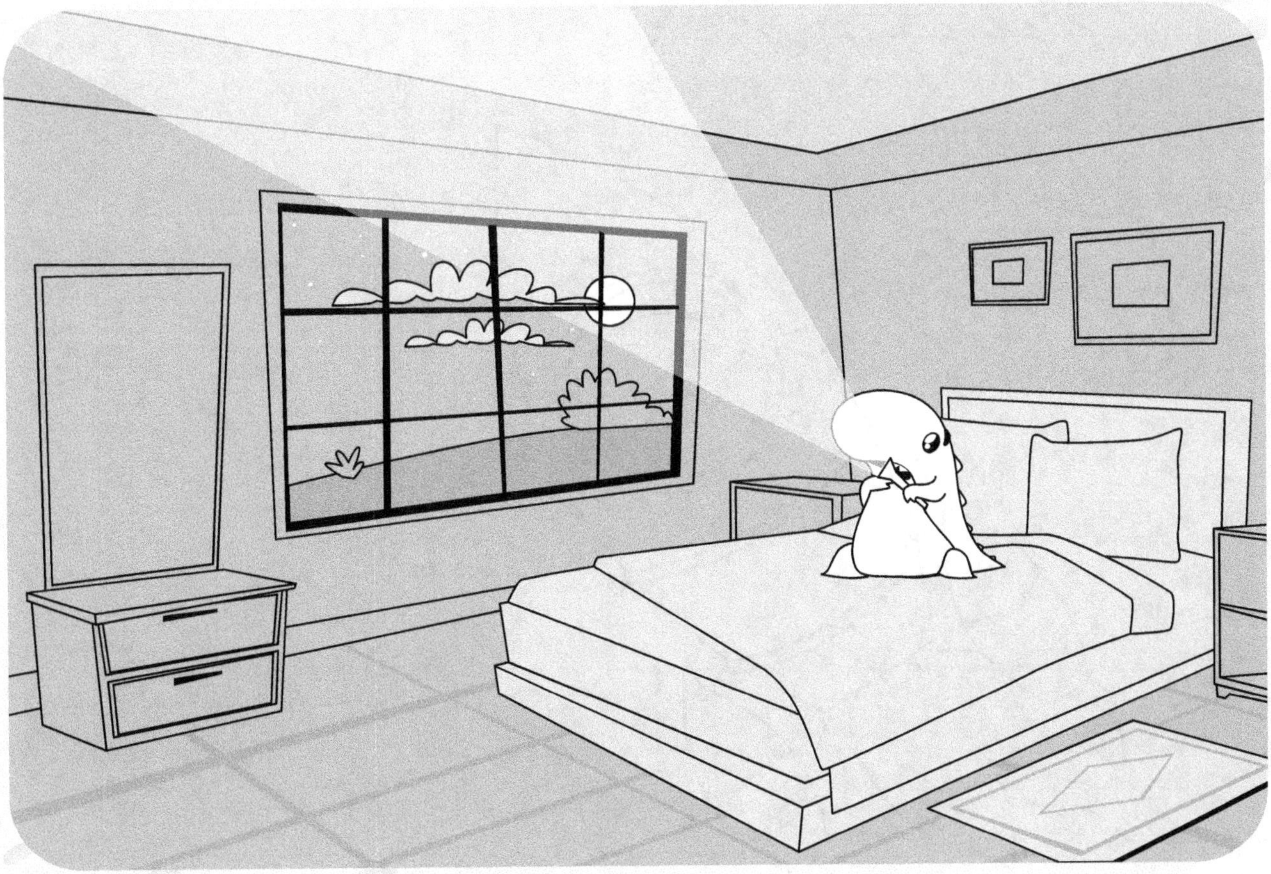

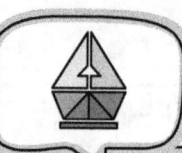
Follow-Up Questions:

1. Write a short summary below that explains how the simulation represents the stars only being visible at night.

....

....

....

....

....

....

....

....

....

Yesterday, you simulated the stars during the day and at night. Today, you will reflect on all that you've learned this week about the patterns of the stars.

Directions: Read and answer each question below.

1. What pattern did you notice in the stars?

2. Why were you able to see the star (flashlight) when the lights were out?

3. Why can we not see the stars during the day?

4. What objects in the sky are visible only during the day?

5. What objects in the sky are visible only at night?

6. What is one new thing you learned this week about the stars?

Earth & Space Science

Seasonal Patterns on Earth

1-ESS1-2

Make observations at different times of year to relate the amount of daylight to the time of year.

ARGOPREP

Directions: Read the text below. Then answer the questions that follow.

"The Four Seasons

The four seasons are winter, spring, summer and fall. Each of these seasons last for about three months and are known for different types of weather. The seasons change because of the way the Earth orbits, or moves around, the Sun. When the Earth is tilted closer to the Sun, it is warmer (spring or summer) on that side of the planet. At that same time, the other half of Earth is tilted further away from the Sun, making it cooler (fall or winter)."

1. The seasons change as the Earth orbits the Sun.

   A. True
   B. False

2. Each season lasts about:

   A. 2 months
   B. 3 months
   C. 4 months
   D. 5 months

3. There are four different seasons.

   A. True
   B. False

4. Each season has different:

   A. Weather
   B. Amounts of sunlight
   C. All of the above

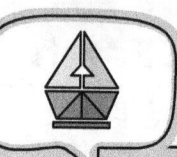
Yesterday, you learned some basic information about the four seasons. Today, you will explore this concept more in-depth.

Directions: Complete the table below by drawing a picture in each box, showing what the weather is like during each of the four seasons where you live.

Winter	Spring
Summer	**Fall**

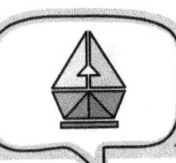
Yesterday, you drew pictures that showed the weather during each of the four seasons where you live. Today, you will learn more about the relationship between the seasons and the amount of daylight at different times throughout the year.

Directions: Using your pictures from yesterday, answer the questions that follow.

1. List a few different activities that could be done during each season.

   Winter: ....

   Spring: ....

   Summer: ....

   Fall: ....

2. Describe how nature (plants, trees, flowers) looks different during each season.

   Winter: ....

   Spring: ....

   Summer: ....

   Fall: ....

3. Have you ever noticed any differences in the amount of daylight during different seasons? If so, describe.

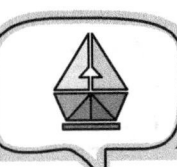
You have spent several days learning about, exploring and explaining the differences between each of the four seasons. Today, you will experiment with this content to learn more about the relationship between the seasons and the amount of daylight at different times throughout the year.

Materials:

1. Internet access or books about the sun and/or seasons

Procedure:

1. Using the internet or books, research how the amount of daylight changes throughout the year.
2. Complete the table below, using the information you find.

Date	Observation of the Sun	Amount of Daylight (in hours)
January 1		
April 20		
July 1		
October 20		

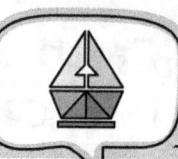
Yesterday, you researched the amount of daylight and position of the Sun at different times throughout the year. Today, you will draw conclusions about these concepts based on what you have learned this week.

Directions: Read and answer each question below.

1. What did you notice about the position of the Sun in the sky throughout the year?

2. What did you notice about the amount of daylight during each season?

3. What conclusions can you draw about the position of the Sun, the amount of daylight hours and each of the seasons?

4. Write a short paragraph telling which season is your favorite and why.

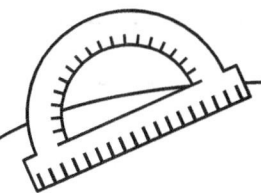

Engineering
Identifying a Problem

K-2-ETS1-1

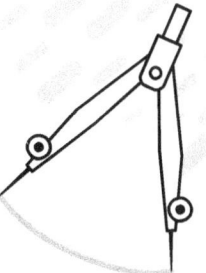

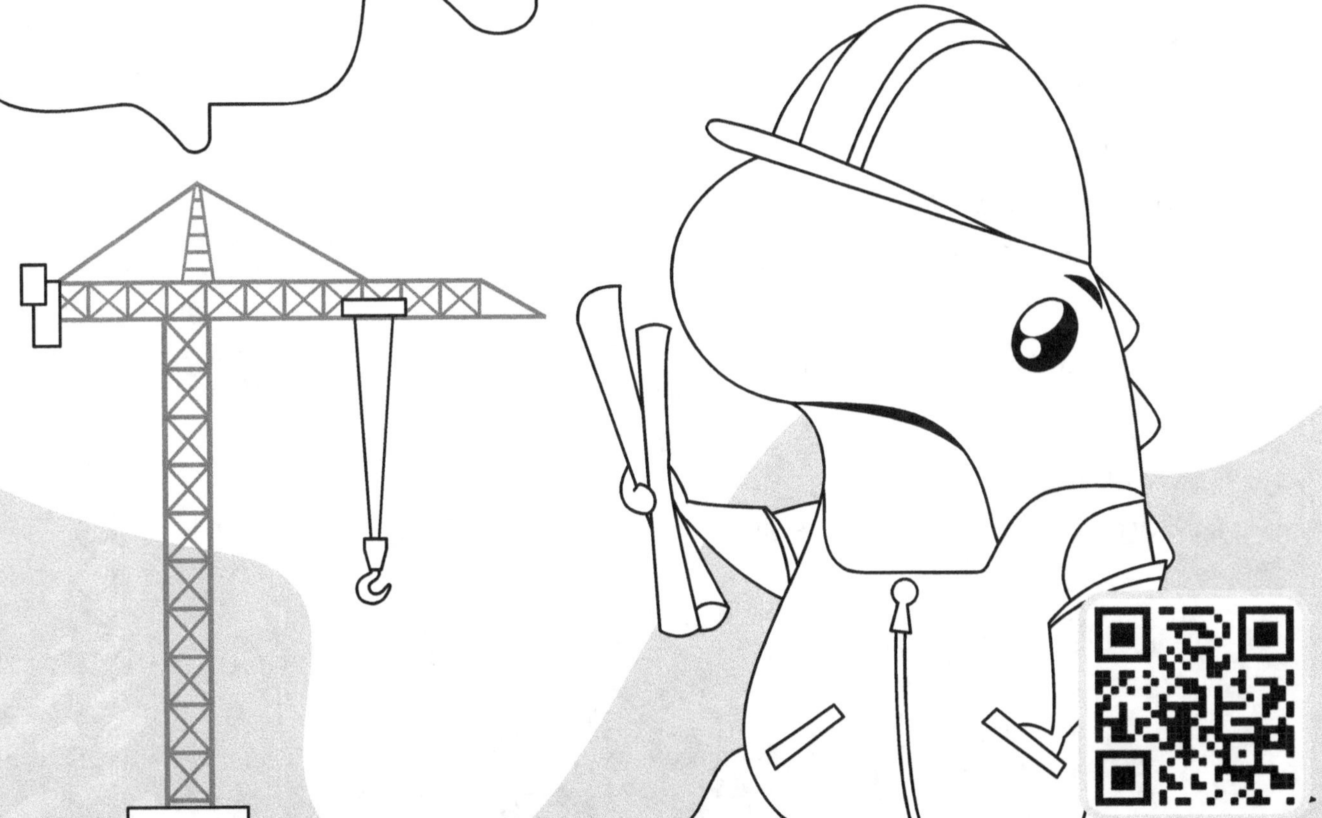

Ask questions, make observations and gather information about a situation people want to change to define a simple problem that can be solved through the development of a new or improved object or tool.

ARGOPREP

Directions: Read the text below. Then answer the questions that follow.

What is Engineering?

Engineering is the process of designing, creating and building things using math and science. An engineer, or person who does the engineering, makes observations, asks questions and collects data in order to figure out the best way to build something. Engineers also solve problems by designing a product or system as a solution to the problem. There are lots of different types of engineers. Some engineers design buildings, roadways or cities while others work with computers or electricity.

1. Engineers use math and science in their jobs.

   A. True

   B. False

2. Engineers:

   A. Make observations

   B. Ask questions

   C. Collect data

   D. All of the above

3. Engineers only build buildings.

   A. True

   B. False

4. Engineers are problem solvers.

   A. True

   B. False

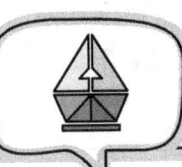
Yesterday, you learned some basic information about engineering. Today, you will explore this concept more in-depth by making observations in order to identify a problem that could be solved.

Directions: Using your own observations of the world, brainstorm a list of problems you notice or situations you would like to change. This could be anything; it does not have to be a problem that you can realistically solve on your own.

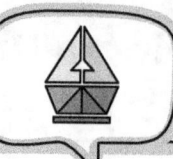
Yesterday, you made observations of situations you would like to change or problems you have noticed. Today, you will dig deeper by brainstorming questions that could be asked in order to identify a problem that could be solved.

Directions: Create a list of questions you could ask various people in your family and/or community about a real-life situation they would like to change. Your goal is to identify a small problem that people have in everyday life and eventually design a solution to that problem.

1. ....

....

....

2. ....

....

....

3. ....

....

....

4. ....

....

....

5. ....

....

....

....

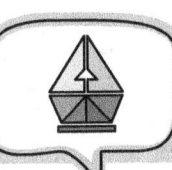
Yesterday, you brainstormed questions you could ask people in order to identify a problem that needs to be solved. Today, you will actually survey people in your family and/or community, using the questions you created.

Directions: Survey 3-5 people in your family and/or community, using the questions you created yesterday. Summarize their responses below.

Person Interviewed	Response Summary

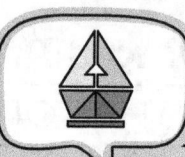
Yesterday, you surveyed people in your family and/or community about situations they would like to see changed. Today, you will analyze all the data you have compiled this week and identify a problem to solve in the coming weeks.

Directions: Read and answer each question below.

1. What were the most common problems that people identified in the survey?

   ....

   ....

   ....

2. Was there agreement among people you surveyed on what problem should be solved?

   ....

   ....

   ....

3. What problem or situation have you identified to solve?

   ....

   ....

   ....

   ....

   ....

   ....

   ....

Engineering
Developing a Solution

K-2-ETS1-1

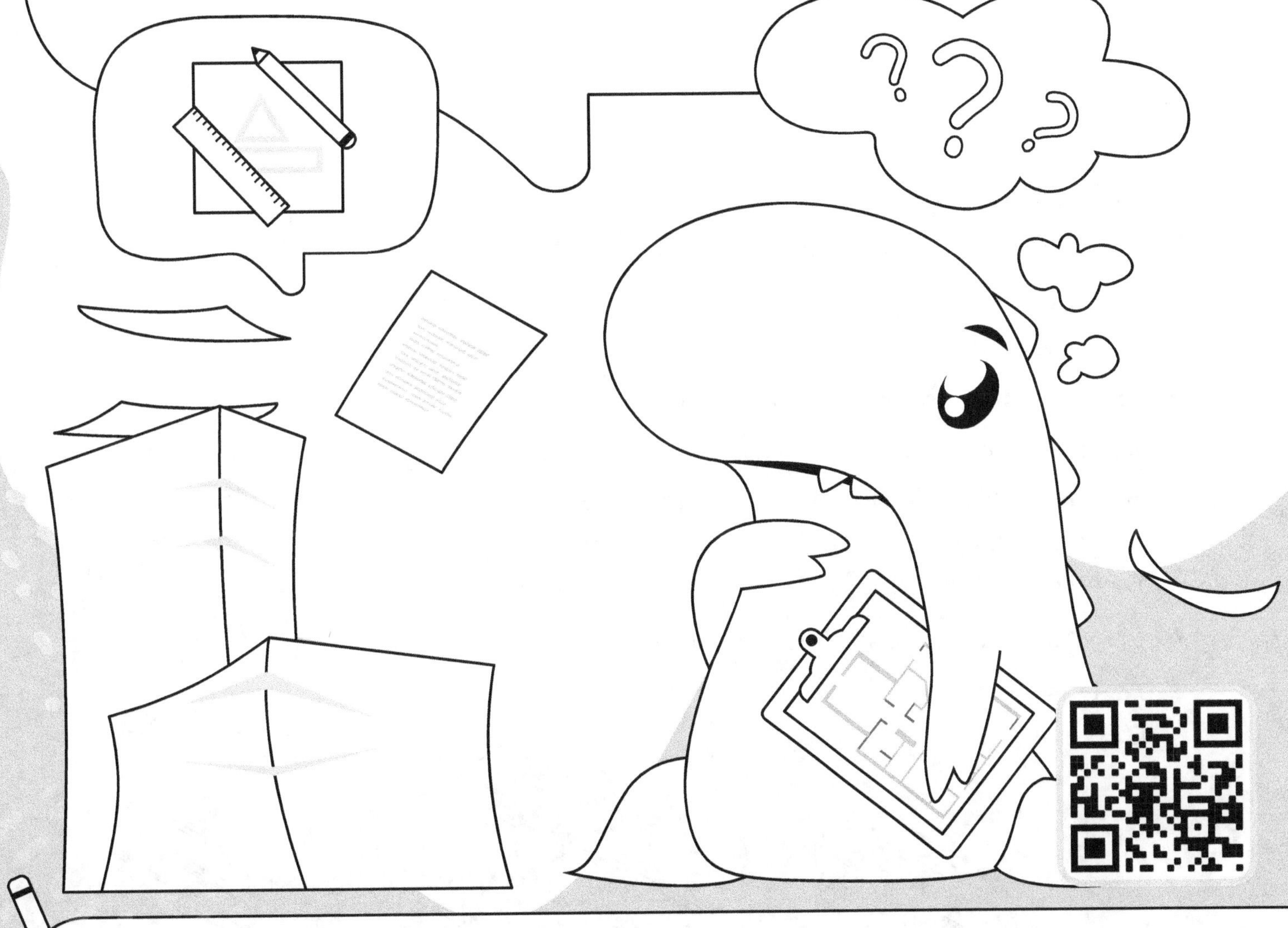

Ask questions, make observations and gather information about a situation people want to change to define a simple problem that can be solved through the development of a new or improved object or tool.

ARGOPREP

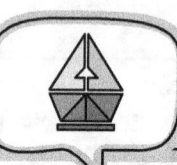
Directions: Read the text below. Then answer the questions that follow.

What is a Solution?

Engineering is the process of designing, creating and building things using math and science. Engineers design solutions to everyday problems. A solution is a way to fix a problem. For instance, a civil engineer may design a roadway that goes around a park, in order to keep playing children safe. Another engineer might design and build a bridge that safely takes people and cars across a river. Engineering is a very important job!

1. Engineers solve all kinds of problems.

   A. True
   B. False

2. There are lots of different types of engineers.

   A. True
   B. False

3. Engineers are important because:

   A. They design safe roadways.
   B. They build bridges to help us get across rivers.
   C. They design and build safe skyscrapers.
   D. All of the above

4. Engineers do not use math or science.

   A. True
   B. False

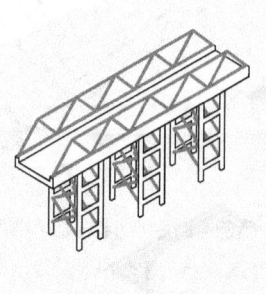
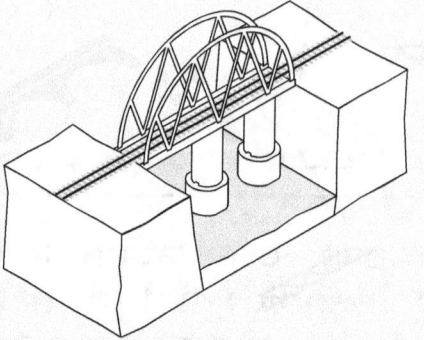
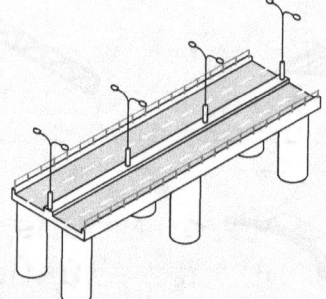

Yesterday, you learned some basic information about designing solutions to problems. Today, you will explore this concept more in-depth by brainstorming possible solutions to the problem you identified last week.

Directions: Brainstorm a list of solutions that could be used to solve the problem you identified last week. This could be anything; it does not have to be a solution that is realistic for you to implement.

Problem:

....

....

Possible Solutions:

....

....

....

....

....

....

....

....

....

....

....

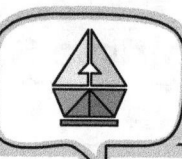
Yesterday, you made a list of possible solutions to your problem. Today, you will dig deeper by brainstorming questions that could be asked of others in order to identify the best possible solution to your problem.

Directions: Create a list of questions you could ask various people in your family and/or community about your list of possible solutions. Your goal is to identify a solution to the problem that people think might work.

1. ....

....

2. ....

....

3. ....

....

4. ....

....

5. ....

....

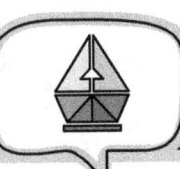
Yesterday, you brainstormed questions you could ask people in order to identify the best possible solution to your problem. Today, you will actually survey people in your family and/or community, using the questions you created.

Directions: Survey 3-5 people in your family and/or community, using the questions you created yesterday. Summarize their responses below.

Person Interviewed	Response Summary

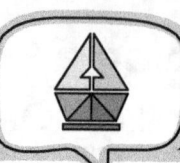
Yesterday, you surveyed people in your family and/or community about possible solutions to your problem. Today, you will analyze all the data you have compiled this week and identify the best solution to your problem.

Directions: Read and answer each question below.

1. What were the solutions people thought might not work?

....

....

....

2. Was there agreement among people you surveyed on what solution you should use?

....

....

....

3. What solution do you plan to use?

....

....

....

....

....

....

Engineering
Designing a Solution

K-2-ETS1-2

Develop a simple sketch, drawing or physical model to illustrate how the shape of an object helps it function as needed to solve a given problem.

ARGOPREP

Directions: Read the text below. Then answer the questions that follow.

What Does it Mean to Design Something?

Engineering is the process of designing, creating and building things using math and science. To design something means to create a plan and then use that plan to build a structure or other project. When engineers design buildings, cities and machines, they make a clear plan before starting. It is very important to have a goal in mind for what the final product looks like or is able to do.

1. Engineers always begin with a plan.

   A. True

   B. False

2. Engineers usually don't have a goal in mind when they begin a project.

   A. True

   B. False

3. To design something means:

   A. To complete a project

   B. To set a goal

   C. To create a plan and build something from that plan

   D. To use math and science

4. A plan is used as a guide for building a project.

   A. True

   B. False

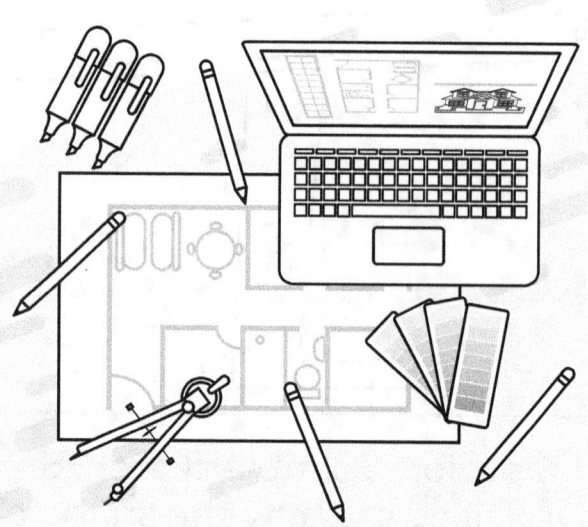

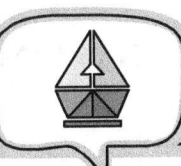
Yesterday, you learned some basic information about how engineers plan for and design solutions to problems. Today, you will explore this concept more in-depth by identifying the final goal for your project.

Directions: Think about the problem and solution you have identified. What is the goal of your project? Answer the questions below.

1. Identify the problem:

_____

_____

_____

2. Identify the solution:

_____

_____

_____

3. What is the goal of your project? What should your design be able to do?

_____

_____

_____

_____

_____

_____

_____

_____

_____

_____

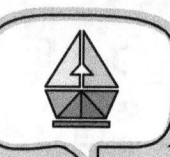
Yesterday, you identified the final goal of your project. Today, you will begin to brainstorm possible plans for the solution you identified last week.

Directions: : Brainstorm a variety of ways the solution you identified last week could be built. This could be a list of materials that could be used or sketches of possible plans for building your project. Use the space below.

Yesterday, you made a list of possible plans for the solution to your problem. Today, you will choose the best idea or combination of ideas from yesterday and begin to design your project.

Directions: Sketch your final design below. Label any important parts, if necessary.

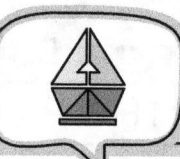
Yesterday, you finalized your project plan. Today, you will elaborate on and explain how your project will work.

Directions: Read and answer each question below.

1. Describe your plan for your project.

....

....

....

2. What materials will you need to design your project?

....

....

....

3. How will your design solve the problem you identified?

....

....

....

....

....

....

....

....

Engineering

Building & Testing Your Solution

K-2-ETS1-3

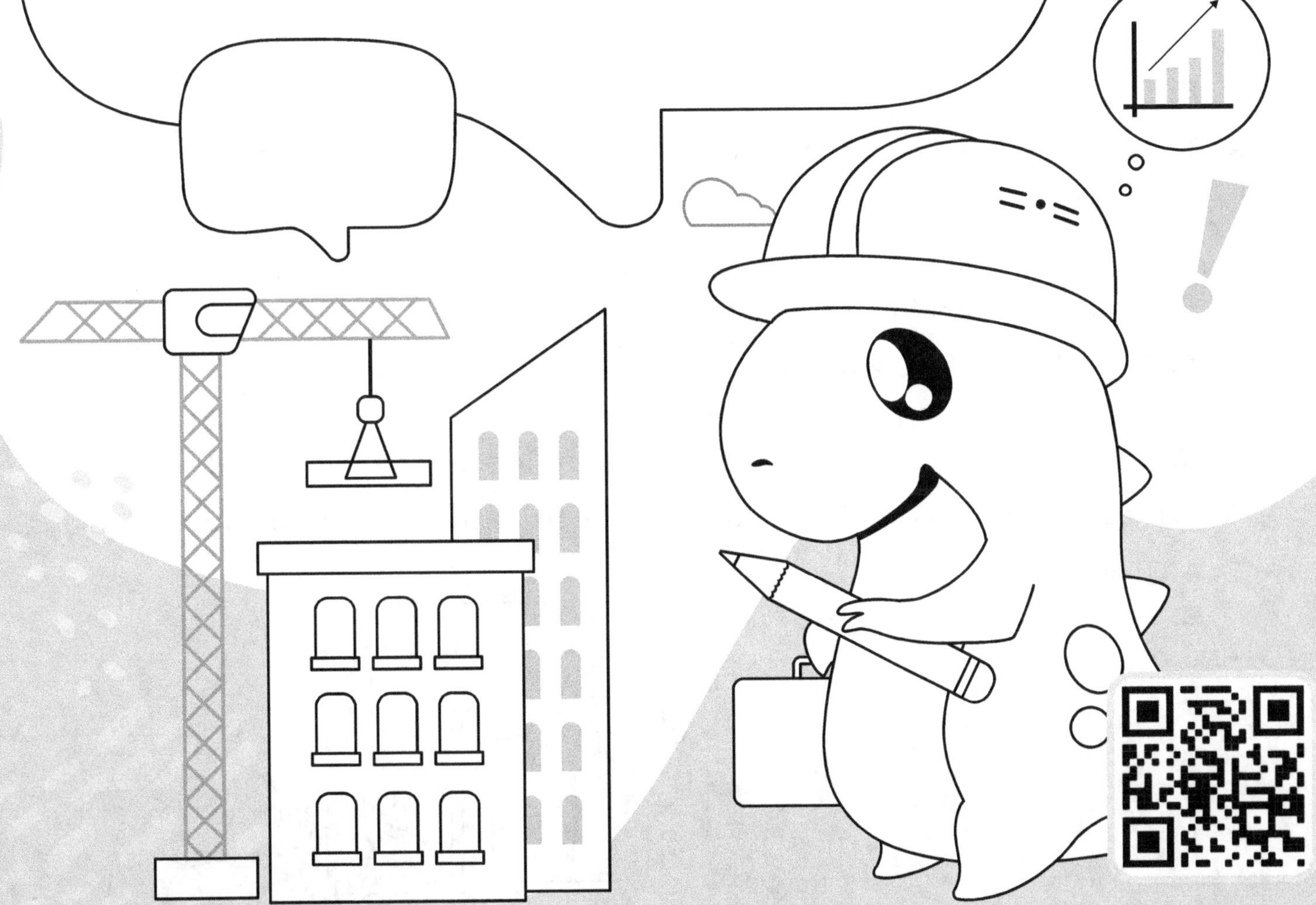

Analyze data from tests of two objects designed to solve the same problem to compare the strengths and weaknesses of how each performs.

ARGOPREP

Directions: Read the text below. Then answer the questions that follow.

How Do Engineers Test Their Designs?

Engineering is the process of designing, creating and building things using math and science. After building something based on their plans, engineers must test their designs to find out if they work the way they should. During testing, engineers might also decide to make changes to their design so that it works even better. This is a very important step in the process.

1. Engineers sometimes test their designs.

   A. True

   B. False

2. Testing a design is an important part of the engineering process.

   A. True

   B. False

3. The purpose of testing their design is:

   A. To find out if it works correctly

   B. To help them improve their design

   C. Both a and b

4. Sometimes designs don't work and engineers have to start over with their plans.

   A. True

   B. False

Engineering: Building & Testing Your Solution

EXPLORING THE TOPIC

Yesterday, you learned about the importance of testing out your design. Today, you will explore this concept more in-depth by actually building your project and preparing it for testing.

Directions: Think back to the project plan sketch you created last week. Today, you will gather all the necessary materials and actually build your project. Then, answer the questions below.

1. What materials did you use to build your design?

2. Does your actual design look like the sketch you created last week?

3. Did you have to make any changes to your design as you were building it? If so, why?

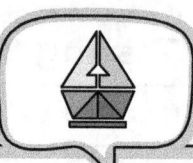
Yesterday, you built your design according to the plans you have created over the past couple of weeks. Today, you will explain how your design should work and how it should solve the problem you identified.

Directions: Answer the questions below.

1. What was the problem you identified?

....

....

....

....

2. What was the solution you identified?

....

....

....

....

....

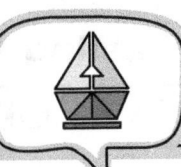
3. How does your design solve the problem?

....

....

....

....

4. How should your design work?

....

....

....

....

5. Can you think of any problems your design might have?

....

....

....

....

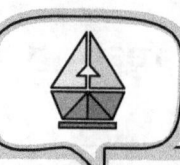
Yesterday, you explained how your design should work to solve the identified problem. Today, you will test it out to determine if it actually works.

Directions: Answer the questions below.

1. Explain how you tested your design.

....

....

....

....

....

....

....

....

2. Was your test a:

   A. Success

   B. Failure

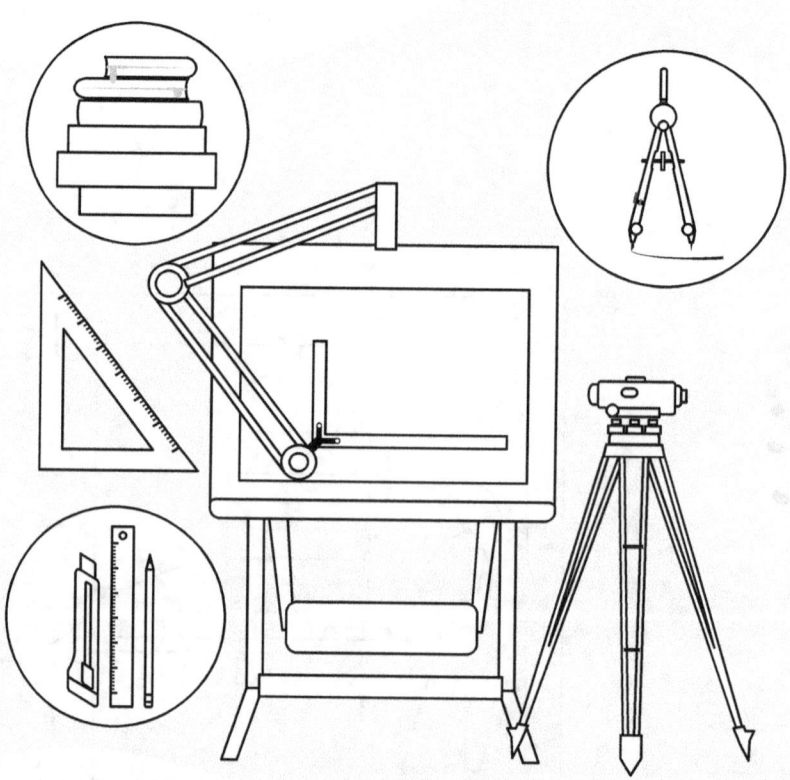

Yesterday, you tested your design. Today, you will reflect on the testing and evaluate how your design worked.

Directions: Read and answer each question below.

1. Did your design work? Why or why not?

2. Do changes need to be made to the design? If so, describe what changes need to be made.

3. Did your design successfully solve the problem you identified? Explain.

WEEK 20

Engineering

Evaluating Solutions

K-2-ETS1-3

Analyze data from tests of two objects designed to solve the same problem to compare the strengths and weaknesses of how each performs.

ARGOPREP

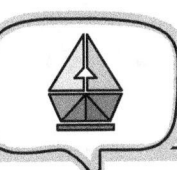
Directions: Read the text below. Then answer the questions that follow.

Evaluating Designs

Testing designs is an important part of an engineer's job. Testing helps the engineer to find out if their design works the way it should or if changes need to be made to improve it. Engineers can then use the testing from different designs to evaluate, or decide, which one works best to solve the problem they have identified.

1. Engineers should always test their designs.

    A. True

    B. False

2. Evaluating different designs is part of an engineer's job.

    A. True

    B. False

3. To evaluate different designs means:

    A. To test them

    B. To make changes to them

    C. To test them and decide which one works best

    D. To build them

4. Sometimes designs have to be changed so they work better.

    A. True

    B. False

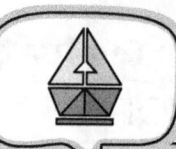
Yesterday, you learned about the importance of testing and evaluating your design. Today, you will explore this concept more in-depth by rebuilding your project, based on the testing you did last week.

Directions: Think back to the reflective questions you answered last week. Today, you will gather all the necessary materials to rebuild your project, making the changes you listed last week. Then, answer the questions below.

1. What materials did you use to rebuild your design?

....

....

....

2. How is your design different from your original design?

....

....

....

3. Did you have to make any additional changes to your design as you were building it? If so, why?

....

....

....

Yesterday, you rebuilt your design according to the testing you did last week. Today, you will test out your redesign to determine if it actually works.

Directions: Test your design. Then, answer the questions below.

1. Explain how you tested your design.

_____

_____

_____

_____

_____

_____

_____

_____

_____

_____

_____

2. Was your test a:

A. Success

B. Failure

Yesterday, you tested your redesign to find out if it worked. Today, you will explain the strengths and weaknesses of each of your designs.

Directions: Answer the questions below.

1. What are the strengths of your original design?

   ....

   ....

   ....

2. What are the weaknesses of your original design?

   ....

   ....

   ....

3. What are the strengths of your redesign?

   ....

   ....

   ....

4. What are the weaknesses of your redesign?

   ....

   ....

   ....

   ....

   ....

   ....

   ....

Yesterday, you evaluated your redesign. Today, you will reflect on the data you've collected and compare the two designs you created.

Directions: Read and answer each question below.

1. Which design worked best? Why?

....

....

....

2. Do changes still need to be made to the design? If so, describe what changes need to be made.

....

....

....

3. Did your design successfully solve the problem you identified? Explain.

....

....

....

....

ANSWER
KEYS

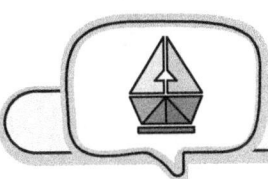
Week 1

Day 1

1. D

2. D

3. C

Day 2

1. Yes

2. Yes

3. Yes

Day 3

1. Plucking the rubber band caused it to vibrate which created sound waves that traveled through the air to your ears.

2. Tapping the spoons together caused vibrations which created sound waves that traveled through the water. You are able to hear the sound through the plastic water bottle that is underwater.

3. Talking into the paper cup caused vibrations which created sound waves that traveled through the string to the other end of the telephone where it changed back to sounds that could be heard.

Day 4

1. Answers will vary, but the louder your voice is when recording, the larger the sound waves are.

Day 5

1. The sound waves were small when recording in a quiet voice.

2. The sound waves were big when recording in a loud voice.

3. The quieter the sound, the smaller the sound wave. The louder the sound, the larger the sound wave.

4. A

5. Vocal cords vibrate when a person speaks which creates sound waves.

6. Answers will vary.

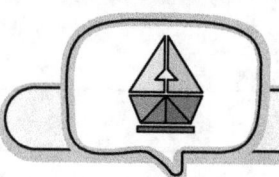

Answer Key

Week 2

Day 1

1. True
2. True
3. False
4. True
5. False

Day 3

1. Answers will vary.
2. Answers will vary.

Day 4

All answers will vary.

Day 5

All answers will vary.

Day 2

Table: answers will vary.

1. Answers will vary.
2. Answers will vary.

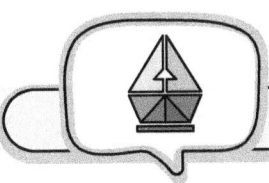

Answer Key

Week 3

Day 1

1. False

2. A

3. B

4. D

Day 2

Table: answers will vary.

1. Yes.

Day 3

1. Answers will vary, but very few objects should be visible.

2. Answers will vary, but many more objects should be visible.

3. We need light to be able to see objects clearly.

4. Because you are unable to see objects clearly in a very dark room. When the lights are turned on, however, you are able to observe many more objects.

5. Answers will vary.

Day 4

1. Answers will vary.

2. Answers will vary.

Day 5

1. You must poke holes on opposite sides of the box, as well as on the top of the box. Shine the flashlight through the hole on the top of the box while looking through one of the holes on the side of the box.

2. Light travels in a straight line so it's important that the holes are placed in certain spots on the box in order to illuminate the object.

3. Light is necessary to illuminate objects so they can be seen.

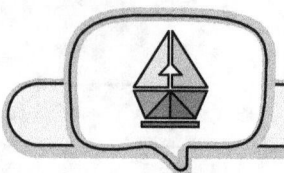

Week 4

Day 1

1. False

2. True

3. A

4. B

Day 2

Table: answers will vary.

Day 3

Table: answers will vary.

Day 4

Table: opaque (1), translucent (3), transparent (5), reflective (1), all other answers will vary.

Day 5

1. The transparent material allowed the most amount of light through.

2. Answers will vary.

3. The opaque and reflective objects blocked or reflected the light, resulting in the least amount of light passing through.

4. Answers will vary.

5. Answers will vary.

6. Answers will vary.

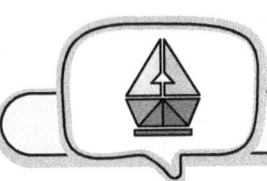

Answer Key

Week 5

Day 1

1. False

2. True

3. True

4. True

5. False

Day 2

Table: answers will vary.

1. Answers will vary.

2. Answers will vary.

Day 3

1. Answers will vary.

2. Answers will vary.

3. Answers will vary.

Day 4

All answers will vary.

Day 5

All answers will vary.

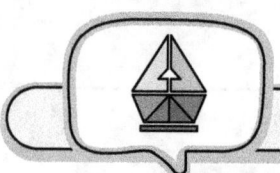

Week 6

Day 1

1. B

2. C

3. D

4. C

Day 2

Table: answers will vary.

Day 3

Table: answers will vary.

Day 4

Table: answers will vary.

Day 5

All answers will vary.

Week 7

Day 1

1. D

2. D

3. True

Day 2

Table: answers will vary.

Day 3

Table: answers will vary.

Day 4

Table: answers will vary.

Day 5

All answers will vary.

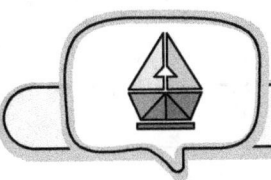

Week 8

Day 1

1. External parts help a plant grow, reproduce and survive in their environment.

2. External parts help an animal find food, adapt to its environment and hide from predators in nature.

3. A

Day 2

Table: answers will vary.

Day 3

Table: answers will vary.

Day 4

All answers will vary.

Day 5

All answers will vary.

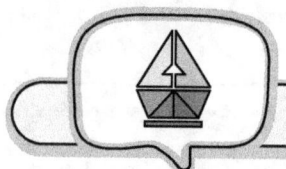

Answer Key

Week 9

Day 1

1. True

2. D

3. B

4. C

Day 2

1. Answers will vary.

2. Baby birds need food, water, shelter and protection from predators. They also need to learn to fly.

3. Parents help care for their offspring by building a nest to keep baby birds safe, gathering food and bringing it back to the nest, protecting them from predators and teaching them to fly.

4. Baby birds communicate their needs by chirping and making other vocal sounds.

5. Parents respond to chirps by providing baby birds with the things they need (food, water, protection, etc.).

Day 3

1. It is important that parents care for their offspring in nature so that their needs are met and they are able to survive in their environment.

2. Answers will vary.

Day 4

1. Baby birds and human babies are similar in that they have survival needs and are unable to care for themselves on their own. They need their parents to help them survive and communicate their needs by making noise.

2. Bird parents and human parents are similar in that they love and care for their offspring and provide them the things they need to survive.

Day 5

All answers will vary.

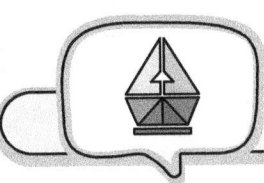

Answer Key

Week 10

Day 1

1. True

2. D

3. A

4. False

Day 3

1. No

2. Answers will vary.

3. Answers will vary.

4. Answers will vary.

5. Answers will vary.

Day 4

Table: answers will vary.

Day 5

All answers will vary.

Day 2

All answers will vary.

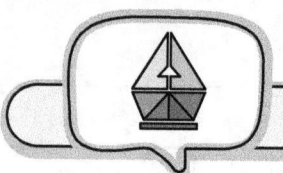

Week 11

Day 1

1. D
2. True
3. B
4. False

Day 2

1. Universe
2. Solar system
3. Planets
4. Moon
5. Galaxy

Day 3

1. All the planets (Mercury, Venus, Earth, Mars, Jupiter, Saturn, Uranus, Neptune), the Sun, moon and stars.
2. The Milky Way
3. There are 2 trillion galaxies in the universe.
4. All answers may vary.

Day 4

1. The slime represents the universe. It stretches and expands just as the universe is expanding.
2. The glitter in the slime represents the trillions of galaxies in the universe.

Day 5

All answers will vary.

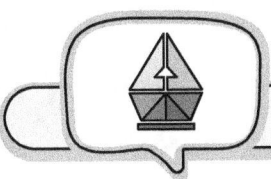
Week 12

Day 1

1. True

2. D

3. C

4. False

Day 2

Table: Morning - Sun is low in the eastern sky. It is daytime.

Afternoon - Sun is high in the eastern sky. It is daytime.

Evening - Sun is high in the western sky. It is daytime.

Night - Sun is low in the western sky or cannot be seen. It is nighttime.

1. The Sun moved across the sky throughout the day, giving off different amounts of light.

2. Answers will vary.

Day 3

1. Yes

2. The Sun was not moving, but it appeared to because the Earth is constantly spinning.

3. As the Earth spins, it makes the Sun appear to move across the sky. When the Sun is shining light on the part of Earth where you live, it is day. When the part of Earth where you live is facing away from the Sun, it is night.

Day 4

1. All answers will vary.

Day 5

1. Yes, the pattern of the Sun can be predicted from day to day. The Sun rises in the east and sets in the west. We have different amounts of light on Earth, depending on where the Sun is in the sky.

2. The Earth rotates, causing half of the planet to receive light from the Sun (daytime) and the other half to be facing away from the Sun (nighttime).

3. We cannot see the Sun at night because our part of the Earth is facing away from the Sun.

4. We usually cannot see the moon during the day because the light from the Sun is too bright or because our part of the Earth is facing away from the moon.

5. Answers will vary.

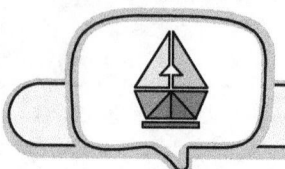

Week 13

Day 1

1. False

2. C

3. A

4. B

Day 2

Table: Answers will vary.

1. The moon looked slightly different each night. We were able to see more/less of its entire shape each night.

2. Answers will vary.

Day 3

1. Answers may vary.

2. The moon was not changing shape, but it appeared to because the sun was only shining on parts of the moon each night.

3. As the moon orbits the Earth, it reflects different amounts of sun. The part of the moon that is lit by the sun is visible at night.

Day 4

1. All answers will vary.

Day 5

1. Yes, the pattern of the moon can be predicted from day to day. The phases of the moon always occur in the same order over the same amount of time.

2. The moon orbits around the Earth, reflecting different amounts of light from the Sun.

3. We cannot see the moon during the day because the light from the Sun is brighter than the light from the moon.

4. Answers will vary.

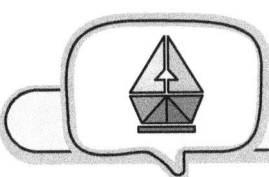
Week 14

Day 1

1. False

2. D

3. True

4. C

Day 2

Table: Answers will vary.

1. During the day, the only visible star is the sun.

2. At night, many stars can be seen in the sky.

Day 3

1. Answers may vary.

2. No, the stars did not disappear during the day. The light from the Sun is so bright that we cannot see them during the day.

3. Some stars appear brighter than others at night because they are closer to Earth than the ones that are dimmer.

Day 4

1. All answers will vary.

Day 5

1. The pattern of the stars is that they can be seen during the nighttime but not during the day.

2. You are able to see the star when the lights were out because there was nothing in the sky giving off more light than the stars.

3. You cannot see the stars during the day because the light from the Sun is too bright.

4. The Sun.

5. The moon and stars.

6. Answers will vary.

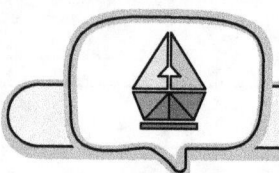

Week 15

Day 1

1. True

2. B

3. True

4. C

Day 2

Table: Answers will vary.

Day 3

1. Answers may vary, depending upon your region.

2. Answers may vary, depending upon your region.

3. Answers may vary.

Day 4

Table: January 1 - the Sun is low in the sky, fewer daylight hours

April 20 - the Sun is a bit higher in the sky, daylight hours increasing

July 1 - the Sun is high in the sky, more daylight hours

October 20 - the Sun is a bit lower in the sky, daylight hours decreasing.

Day 5

1. The Sun is higher in the sky during the summer months and lower in the sky during the winter months.

2. There are more daylight hours during the summer months than the winter months.

3. Answers will vary.

4. Answers will vary.

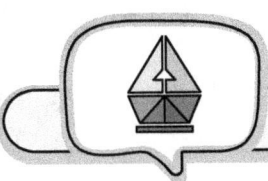

Week 16

Day 1

1. True

2. D

3. False

4. True

Day 2

All answers will vary.

Day 3

All answers will vary.

Day 4

All answers will vary.

Day 5

All answers will vary.

Week 17

Day 1

1. True

2. True

3. D

4. False

Day 2

All answers will vary.

Day 3

All answers will vary.

Day 4

All answers will vary.

Day 5

All answers will vary.

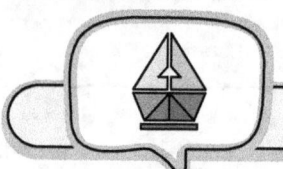
Week 18

Day 1

1. True

2. False

3. C

4. True

Day 2

All answers will vary.

Day 3

All answers will vary.

Day 4

All answers will vary.

Day 5

All answers will vary.

Week 19

Day 1

1. False

2. True

3. C

4. True

Day 2

All answers will vary.

Day 3

All answers will vary.

Day 4

All answers will vary.

Day 5

All answers will vary.

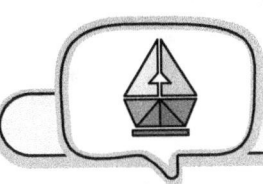

Week 20

Day 1

1. True

2. True

3. C

4. True

Day 3

All answers will vary.

Day 4

All answers will vary.

Day 5

All answers will vary.

Day 2

All answers will vary.

www.ingramcontent.com/pod-product-compliance
Lightning Source LLC
Chambersburg PA
CBHW081329120626
46546CB00011B/3270